U0890184

TO MY LOVE

Lu Ping

A Reasonable Affliction

爱的心灵咒语

[英]威廉·莎士比亚 [爱尔兰]威廉·巴特勒·叶芝 等 著
金培武◎译

南方出版传媒
广东经济出版社
-广州-

图书在版编目（CIP）数据

爱的心灵咒语／（英）威廉·莎士比亚等著；金培武译．—广州：广东经济出版社，2018.1
ISBN 978－7－5454－5917－3

Ⅰ．①爱…　Ⅱ．①威…　②金…　Ⅲ．①爱情诗－诗歌欣赏－英国 ②爱情诗－诗歌欣赏－美国　Ⅳ．①I561．072　②I712．072

中国版本图书馆 CIP 数据核字（2017）第 283684 号

插　　画：阿尔丰斯·穆夏

出 版 人：姚丹林
责任编辑：张晶晶
责任技编：许伟斌
封面设计：何汝清
封面插画（复刻）：夏　佳

《爱的心灵咒语》（Ai de Xinling Zhouyu）
A Reasonable Affliction
（英）威廉·莎士比亚　（爱尔兰）威廉·巴特勒·叶芝　等　著
金培武　译

出版发行	广东经济出版社（广州市环市东路水荫路 11 号 11～12 楼）
经销	全国新华书店
印刷	佛山市浩文彩色印刷有限公司
	（佛山市南海区狮山科技工业园 A 区）
开本	889 毫米×1194 毫米　1/32
印张	8.5　2 插页
字数	100 000 字
版次	2018 年 1 月第 1 版
印次	2018 年 1 月第 1 次
书号	ISBN 978－7－5454－5917－3
定价	39.80 元

如发现印装质量问题，影响阅读，请与承印厂联系调换。
发行部地址：广州市环市东路水荫路 11 号 11 楼
电话：（020）38306055　37601950　邮政编码：510075
邮购地址：广州市环市东路水荫路 11 号 11 楼
电话：（020）37601980　营销网址：**http://www.gebook.com**
广东经济出版社新浪官方微博：**http://e.weibo.com/gebook**
广东经济出版社常年法律顾问：何剑桥律师

目录
CONTENTS

推荐序
PREFACE

杨先顺

（暨南大学新闻与传播学院广告系教授、博士生导师）

青年男子谁个不善钟情？

妙龄女人谁个不善怀春？

这是我们人性中的至圣至神。

许多年之前，当我还在大学一年级的时候，偶尔在学校图书馆遇到歌德的《少年维特之烦恼》，便借回宿舍一口气读了下去，竟然感慨万千，无语凝噎。而其中的题诗更是让我沉浸其中，久久不能自拔，我第一次感受到了爱情诗的魔力和魅力！当时心想人类大约有两样最美妙的东西吧：一是让人荡气回肠、欲罢不能的爱情；二是优美抒情、如梦如幻的诗歌。如果把二者融为一体，定会创造美轮美奂、至善至美的人间仙境了。正如2400多年前柏拉图所言："在爱情的触摸下，人人皆成诗人。"爱情与诗歌之间有天然的血缘关系：爱情可以将普通人转化为诗人，诗歌可以帮助人们揭示爱情的许多奥秘。诗歌是表现爱情的最完美的文学形式。

自古至今，那些描绘爱情的诗歌佳作总会流芳百世，历久弥新，让人体验到这种情感的高峰与低谷、喜悦与悲苦、期盼与失落。世界最古老的诗集《诗经》就有“关关雎鸠，在河之洲。窈窕淑女，君子好逑”的倾心爱慕的表达。几千年来，情诗连绵不断，同样引起我们现代人的共鸣。清词丽句，脍炙人口的不胜枚举。例如，表现坚贞不渝的，有汉乐府《上邪》：“山无陵，江水为竭，冬雷震震，夏雨雪，天地合，乃敢与君绝！”表现悔恨、无奈与绝望的，有陆游的《钗头凤》：“东风恶，欢情薄。一怀愁绪，几年离索。错错错！”表现几近偏执的恋情的，有元稹的《离思》：“曾经沧海难为水，除却巫山不是云。”表现契入骨髓的悲痛与思念的，有苏轼的《江城子》：“十年生死两茫茫，不思量，自难忘。”道尽世间儿女情长、离愁别绪的，有关汉卿《双调·沉醉东风》：“咫尺的天南地北，霎时间月缺花飞。手执着饯行杯，眼阁着别离泪。”这些千古绝唱，形成了古典文学璀璨瑰丽的宝藏，有待我们深入发掘。

当然，国外爱情诗也有诸多名篇佳作，令人心驰神往。有莎士比亚十四行诗第 116 首的永恒爱情：“爱情不是时间玩物，尽管红颜朱唇 / 终究逃不脱时间弯镰的无情蹂躏：/ 爱情决不会因短促韶华而变更，/ 甚至到厄运边缘也能坚守忠贞。”有勃郎宁夫人的《我该如何爱你》的热烈深沉：“我爱你，伴随呼吸、微笑和泪水，以至整个生命！”有肯明斯的《我将你的心带在身上》的心心相印：“我将你的心带在身上（我把它放在我的心里珍藏），我从未离开过它（无论我去哪里，都有你陪伴在我身旁，我的宝贝）。”有叶芝的《当你老了》的灵魂升华——“多少人爱你快乐优雅的时分，/ 爱你的美丽，无论假意或真情；/ 但有一人爱着你那朝圣者的心灵，/ 爱那日益衰老的脸庞的伤痕”。

然而，相比国内的爱情诗，普通读者对于国外爱情诗的认知和鉴赏就相对少了，其中一个重要原因在于语言的障碍。所幸，我的朋友金培武先生给了我们一个意外的惊喜！

金先生是中国改革开放以来第一代广告管理者，他从业30多年，曾经利用业余时间潜心编撰，编译一本工具书《营销传播A–Z》，收入1万多个词条，字数150多万字，惶惶然成为鸿篇巨制。他退休后，担任广州市广告行业协会秘书长，不遗余力地推动广告领域学界与业界的紧密合作，因此，我们得以熟悉而成为好朋友。他认真负责的工作作风，做事力求达到极致的执着精神，给我留下深刻印象。前几个月，他把这本译诗稿拿给我，特邀请我作序，我欣然应承。此时，我才知他是个酷爱文学的前辈。我拜读了他的部分译作，感觉又回到青春时代。爱情恒久远，经典永留传！感谢他给了我重温爱情、品味佳作的机会。

早在30多年前，金先生就是一个狂热的英文诗的发烧友，20世纪80年代他曾小试牛刀，发表了两篇译作。还一度在忙碌之余阅读英文诗，让美丽的文字和美妙的情感纾解工作的压力和紧张的神经。难能可贵的是他一直没有放弃与爱情诗的“幽会”，当有一天他赋闲在家，终于有机会和“她”公开恋情，完成夙愿，并诞生下这美丽鲜活的婴孩——《爱的心灵咒语》。

这本爱情诗集是金先生呕心沥血之作，从他收集、积累的众多资料中精选出的98首英语爱情诗。于读者而言，我想会有如下的意义和价值：其一，沙里淘金，精挑细选。信息化时代，面对变化诡谲的海量信息，需要舍弃浮华，把握精髓；需要摒弃杂乱，回归本质。在浩如烟海的爱情诗中，你或许无暇逐一阅读、筛选，但本书译者以独特的感悟为你精选了英语爱情诗的佳作，值得细细品味。其二，丰富细腻，感人至深。经典爱情诗反映爱情的多重性，总有一首诗会引起你的共鸣，无论你正在经历爱情的哪个阶段，无论你是堕入情网或者失恋。我们多数人努力寻找恰当的词语，表白我们的爱情，当你无言以对时，这些诗将会帮助你。每一首诗会给予你爱的力量。其三，用心体验，悉心打磨。译者虽不是专门从事诗歌翻译及其研究的专家，但他以丰富的个人阅历去体验原诗的意境、领悟爱情的真谛，继而字斟句酌、认真推敲，寻找恰当而又传神的汉语表达。读了金先生的译作会有别有洞天的意蕴和想象。正可谓：“养文培武藏深蕴，达意传情译金言！”

AMEN
AINSI SOIT-IL

Sweet Love

William Shakespeare(1564-1616)

Sweet love, renew thy[1] force; be it not said
Thy edge should blunter be than appetite,
Which but today by feeding is allayed,
Tomorrow sharpened in his former might:
So, love, be thou; although today thou fill
Thy hungry eyes even till they wink with fullness,
Tomorrow see again, and do not kill
The spirit of love with a perpetual dullness.
Let this sad interim like the ocean be
Which parts the shore, where two contracted new
Come daily to the banks, that when they see
Return of love, more blest may be the view;
Or call it winter, which being full of care,
Makes summer's welcome, thrice more wished, more rare.

[1] 古英语 thou、thee 是“你”的意思，thy 是“你的”的意思，是 thou 的所有格。thou、thy 和 thee 用于亲近的人之间以及对小孩和地位较低的人说话；ye、your 和 you 用于对地位较高的人或不熟悉的人说话。

甜蜜的爱

［英］威廉·莎士比亚

甜蜜的爱，重新焕发你的活力；
别说你的锋芒比起食欲更迟钝，
只是今天饱餐后暂时感到满意，
明天会与从前一样，馋涎倍增：
爱也是如此；尽管今天你填饱
你的饥饿眼睛，直到眼瘆伤神，
明天又极想见面，千万不要
用永远的麻木扼杀爱的精灵。
让这悲伤的暂别，好像海洋
分隔这两个缔结婚约的新人，
他们每天都要来到海堤眺望，
一旦爱人回归，眼睛闪耀欢欣；
　如不然称作冬天，心中充满忧烦，
　夏天来临，有更多憧憬，更多渴盼。

Let Me Not to Admit

William Shakespeare (1564-1616)

Let me not to the marriage of true minds
Admit impediments. Love is not love
Which alters when it alteration finds,
Or bends with the remover to remove:
O no, it is an ever-fixed mark,
That looks on tempests and is never shaken;
It is the star to every wandering barque,
Whose worth's unknown, although his height be taken.
Love's not time's fool, though rosy lips and cheeks
Within his bending sickle's compass come;
Love alters not with his brief hours and weeks,
But bears it out even to the edge of doom.
   If this be error and upon me proved,
   I never writ, nor no man ever loved.

我不会承认

[英] 威廉·莎士比亚

我不会承认真心实意的结合姻缘
存在各种障碍。如果发现他人摇摆
也随之改变，或者对方移情别恋
而委曲求全，那么，爱就不是真爱：
啊，不！爱情是永远固定的航标，
直面狂风暴雨，永远也不会动摇；
爱情是北极星，将迷途航船引导，
虽然高度可测，价值却无人知晓。
爱情不是时间玩物，尽管红颜朱唇
终究逃不脱时间弯镰的无情蹂躏：
爱情决不会因短促韶华而变更，
甚至到厄运边缘也能坚守忠贞。
　如果这话错误，在我身上得到验证，
　我就从未写过，世上也无真爱的人。

这首在各种选本中选用的频率较高。莎士比亚声明真爱是专一的、真挚的，可以克服任何障碍。如同一颗星是恒定的，指引迷航的船只穿过汹涌的海面，爱情面对重重困难决不动摇。

Love's Philosophy

Percy Bysshe Shelley (1792-1822)

The fountains mingle with the river
And the rivers with the ocean,
The winds of heaven mix forever
With a sweet emotion;
Nothing in the world is single;
All things by a law divine
In one spirit meet and mingle.
Why not I with thine?

See the mountain kiss high heaven
And the waves clasp one another;
No sister-flower would be forgiven
If it disdained its brother;
And the sunlight clasps the earth
And the moonbeams kiss the sea:
What is all this sweet work worth
If thou kiss not me?

爱的哲学

[英] 珀西·比希·雪莱

条条泉水流入江河，
　　奔腾江河与海洋融汇，
天上的风与风交混，
　　彼此感情永远甜蜜；
世上一切不会孤单存在；
　　万物都遵循神圣法则，
相交融合于同一精神，
　　为什么你我不是如此？

看崇山峻岭亲吻蓝天，
　　波浪紧紧拥抱无比亲密；
没有一个姐姐会被谅解，
　　如果她嫌弃自己的弟弟；
柔和月光亲吻着海波，
　　温暖阳光搂抱着大地：
如果你热吻的不是我，
　　这一切甜美又有何价值？

Elizabeth Barrett Browning (1806-1861)

If Thou Must Love Me

If thou must love me, let it be for nought
Except for love's sake only. Do not say,
"I love her for her smile—her look—her way
Of speaking gently,—for a trick of thought
That falls in well with mine, and certes brought
A sense of pleasant ease on such a day"—
For these things in themselves, Beloved, may
Be changed, or change for thee—and love, so wrought,
May be unwrought so. Neither love me for
Thine own dear pity's wiping my cheeks dry—
A creature might forget to weep, who bore
Thy comfort long, and lose thy love thereby!
But love me for love's sake, that evermore
Thou mayst love on, through love's eternity.

如果你真心爱我

［英］伊丽莎白·巴蕾特·勃朗宁

如果你真心爱我，就该为爱而爱，
只是为爱的缘故。请你不要讲，
“我爱她是因为她的微笑——她的模样——
她的语调温柔，——因为思想盘算
与我不谋而合，真正给我带来
这样一天的无比愉快和欢欣”——
这些优点，亲爱的，它们本身
可以变化，或因你而变——这样生成爱，
也可能失去。爱我，也别这样干——
以你亲切的怜悯擦干我的泪痕；
生灵都可能会忘记哭泣，会厌烦
你的长久怜惜，也会厌弃你的爱情！
只是为了爱的缘故爱我，你今后可以
永远地爱下去，这样爱到永生永世。

I Will Tell Thee What It Is to love

Charles Swain (1801-1874)

Love? I will tell thee what it is to love!
It is to build with human thoughts a shrine,
Where Hope sits brooding like a beauteous dove;
Where Time seems young, and Life a thing divine.
All tastes, all pleasures, all desires combine
To consecrate this sanctuary of bliss.
Above, the stars in cloudless beauty shine;
Around, the streams their flowery margins kiss;
And if there's heaven on earth, that heaven is surely this.

Yes, this is love, the steadfast and the true,
The immortal glory which hath never set;
The best, the brightest boom the heart e'er knew:
Of all life's sweets the very sweetest yet!
O' who but can recall the eve they met
To breathe, in some green walk, their first young vow?
While summer flowers with moonlight dews were wet,
And winds sighed soft around the mountain's brow,
And all was rapture then which is but memory now!

我会告诉你爱情是什么

[英] 查尔斯·斯温

爱情？我将告诉你爱情是什么！
它是用人类思想建造的殿堂，
希望坐着沉思像美丽的白鸽；
时间似乎年轻，生命充满圣光，
所有品味、快乐和欲望相结合，
奉献给这个避难的极乐之邦。
天上，星星在无云的美中闪烁光芒；
周围，溪流拥吻着鲜花装饰的沿岸；
如果人间有天堂，这里就是天堂。

是的，这是爱情，坚定而真实，
永恒的荣耀决不会消沉迷失；
最好的、最光辉的恩惠心上人曾经知道：
这是所有生活甜美之中最甜美！
啊，谁能回忆起他们相遇的前夜，
第一次青春誓言，绿色小道上的低语？
虽然在月光下夏花露珠晶莹欲滴，
风儿萦绕着山巅轻轻地叹息，
一切都欣喜若狂，现在成为美好记忆！

Love

O power of Love, O wondrous mystery!
How is my dark illumined by thy light,
That maketh[1] morning of my gloomy night,
Setting my soul from Sorrow's bondage free
With swift-sent revelation! Yea, I see
Beyond the limitation of my sight
And senses, comprehending now, aright,
Today's proportion to eternity.
Through thee, my faith in God is made more sure,
My searching eyes have pierced the misty veil;
The pain and anguish which stern Sorrow brings
Through thee become more easy to endure.
Love-strong I mount, and heaven's high summit scale;
Through thee, my soul has spread her folded wings.

[1] maketh 是动词 make 的（古典式）第三人称单数直陈式一般现在时变位形式，相当于现代英文的 makes。

爱

［美］卡特莉娜·特拉斯克

哦，爱的力量，哦，奇妙的神秘！
你的光芒如何照亮我的黑夜，
使我黯淡夜晚变成璀璨晨曦，
使我心灵快速得到及时启示，
摆脱悲伤的束缚！是的，我看清
超出我的视野和感觉的樊篱，
现在能够正确无误地理解，
今天永恒爱情的构成比例。
通过你，我更坚定信仰上帝，
我求索的眼睛能洞穿面纱的隐秘；
严酷的悲伤带来创痛和苦恼，
通过你，我变得更容易忍痛含悲。
爱情强大令我攀登天空最高顶峰之上；
通过你，我的心灵展开她收拢的翅膀。

Upon the Sand

Ella Wheeler Wilcox (1850-1919)

All love that has not friendship for its base,
Is like a mansion built upon the sand.
Though brave its walls as any in the land,
And its tall turrets lift their heads in grace;
Though skillful and accomplished artists trace
Most beautiful designs on the every hand,
And gleaming statues in dim niches stand,
And fountains play in some flow'r-hidden place;

Yet, when from the frowning east a sudden gust
Of adverse fate is blown, or sad rains fall
Day in, day out, against its yielding wall,
Lo! The fair structure crumbles to the dust.
Love, to endure life's sorrow and earth's woe,
Needs friendship's solid masonwork below.

在沙上

［美］埃拉·惠勒·威尔科克斯

所有的爱情没有友谊作为基础
就好像高楼大厦建在沙上。
尽管它的墙在大地上无与伦比的壮观，
它的高高塔楼造型优雅且轩昂；
尽管技巧高超的设计师追求
各个方面设计都臻于最佳，
闪光的雕像在暗黑壁龛上挺立，
泉水在某个花朵掩藏的地方迸发：

但是，突然东方一阵狂风呼啸，
时乖命蹇，悲伤的暴雨哗哗落下，
日复一日，对着它的倾圮变形的墙，
看！美丽的构造化为尘土轰然倒塌。
爱情，忍受生活的悲伤和大地的灾难，
需要友谊坚固的基础工程支撑构架。

The Revelation

Coventry Patmore (1823-1896)

An idle poet, here and there,
    Looks round him; but, for all the rest,
The world, unfathomably fair,
    Is duller than a witling's jest.
Love wakes men, once a lifetime each;
    They lift their heavy lids, and look;
And, lo, what one sweet page can teach,
    They read with joy, then shut the book.
And some give thanks, and some blaspheme
    And most forget; but, either way,
That and the Child's unheeded dream
Is all the light of all their day.

启示

［英］考文垂·帕特莫尔

一个懒散诗人，东游西逛，
　环顾四周；对于他人非同寻常，
这个世界，高深莫测的女性，
　比自作聪明的玩笑更荒唐。
爱情唤醒男人，一生一次；
　他们抬起沉重的眼皮观望；
瞧，一张甜蜜的页面可以教导，
　他们快乐阅读，就将书本合上。
有的感恩，有的恶言谩骂，
　多数忘记；但不管怎样，
这与孩子不予理会的梦想一样
都是他们所有日子的亮光。

Sir Philip Sidney (1554-1586)

The Bargain

My true love hath my heart, and I have his,
  By just exchange one for another given:
I hold his dear, and mine he cannot miss,
  There never was a better bargain driven:
    My true love hath my heart, and I have his.

His heart in me keeps him and me in one,
  My heart in him his thoughts and senses guides:
He loves my heart, for once it was his own,
  I cherish his because in me it bides:
    My true love hath my heart, and I have his.

交易

［英］菲利普·西德尼爵士

我的真爱拥有我的心，我也有他的心，
　因为我们刚刚已经交换了彼此的心：
我保存他的爱心，他对我也不能掉以轻心，
　再也没有更好的交易可以促成：
　　我的真爱拥有我的心，我也有他的心。

他的心在我身上，他和我在一起保存，
　我的心在他身上，有他的思想和理智指引：
他爱我的心，这曾经就是他自己的心，
　我珍惜他的心因为它留在我这里：
　　我的真爱拥有我的心，我也有他的心。

西德尼爵士也许是英国伊丽莎白时代的理想的文艺复兴式的人物。他是一个士兵、社会活动家和学者，也是一个有天赋的抒情诗人。《交易》是双方（情人之间）“利益”的更为公平的交换和有趣的考验。

Edna St. Vincent Millay (1892-1950)

Love Is Not All

Love is not all: It is not meat nor drink
Nor slumber nor a roof against the rain;
Nor yet a floating spar to men that sink
And rise and sink and rise and sink again.
Love can not fill the thickened lung with breath
Nor clean the blood, nor set the fractured bone;
Yet many a man is making friends with death
Even as I speak, for lack of love alone.
It well may be that in a difficult hour;
Pinned down by pain and moaning for release,
Or nagged by want past resolution's power,
I might be driven to sell you love for peace,
Or trade the memory of this night for food.
It well may be. I do not think I would.

爱情不是一切

[美] 埃德娜·圣·文森特·米莱

爱情不是一切：它不是佳肴美酒，
不是睡眠也不是遮挡风雨的房顶；
也不是在海上漂泊的帆樯
载着挣扎求生的人浮浮沉沉。
爱情不能深呼吸充满增厚的肺部，
不能清洁血液，也不能壮筋续骨；
更有许多人竟会与死亡结交朋友，
如我所说，是因为缺少爱的眷顾。
很可能是处在一个困难的时刻，
被痛苦所压抑，为解脱而叹气，
或因过去缺少决断力而遭到指责，
可能迫使我以你的爱将宁静换取，
或者为饱餐交换这个夜晚的回忆。
它很可能是。我认为我不至于如此。

米莱的诗经常表现个人爱情和人生的经历感悟，与充满激情放弃一种明智的意识相关。在这首短小锐利的作品中，她衡量激情价值的浪漫感觉与更加务实的担忧，发现有利于向爱情倾斜的平衡。

Love and the Rose

Sir Walter Scott (1771-1832)
[英] 沃尔特·司各特爵士

The rose is fairest when 'tis budding new,
And hope is brightest when it dawns from fears:
The rose is sweetest washed with morning dew,
And love is loveliest when embalmed in tears.
O wilding rose, whom fancy thus endears,
I bid your blossoms in my bonnet wave,
Emblem of hope and love through future years!

爱情与玫瑰

玫瑰在含苞欲放时最美丽，
希望在恐惧中破晓最明艳：
玫瑰因晨露清洗过最芳香，
爱情有泪水浸泡过最可爱。
啊，野玫瑰，印象令人钟爱，
我愿你在我的帽檐边盛开，
作为未来岁月希望和爱情的象征。

GISMONDA
BERNHARDT
THÉATRE DE LA RENAISSANCE
Mucha
IMPRIMERIES LEMERCIER, PARIS.

JOB

Mucha

ÉCLAT DU JOUR

ÉVEIL DU MATIN

Mucha
RÊVERIE DU SOIR

Mucha
REPOS DE LA NUIT

Mucha

Mucha

JOB
Mucha
IMP. F. CHAMPENOIS. 66 Boul.d St Michel. PARIS

Love's Calendar

Thomas Bailey Aldrich (1836-1907)
［美］托马斯·贝利·奥尔德里奇

The Summer comes and the Summer goes;
Wild-flowers are fringing the dusty lanes,
The swallows go darting through fragrant rains,
Then, all of a sudden—it snows.

Dear Heart, our lives so happily flow,
So lightly we heed the flying hours,
We only know Winter is gone—by the flowers,
We only know Winter is come—by the snow.

爱情日历

夏天来了，夏天又走了；
野花装点在尘土飞扬的车道，
燕子飞翔穿过芳香的细雨，
那时，突如其来——下雪了。

亲爱的心上人，我们的生活幸福流畅，
这么轻快，我们只留心这飞逝的钟点，
我们只知道冬天走了——看鲜花开放，
我们只知道冬天来了——看雪片弥漫。

When I Have Fears

John Keats (1795-1821)

When I have fears that I may cease to be
Before my pen has gleaned my teeming brain,
Before high-piled books in charact'ry
Hold like rich garners the full ripened grain;
When I behold, upon the night's starred face
Huge cloudy symbols of a high romance,
And think that I may never live to trace
Their shadows with the magic hand of chance;
And when I feel, fair creature of an hour,
That I shall never look upon thee more,
Never have relish in the faery power
Of unreflecting love!—then on the shore
Of the wide world I stand alone, and think
Till love and Fame to nothingness do sink.

当我害怕

[英] 约翰·济慈

当我害怕，在我停止生命的时刻，
　我的笔尚未记下我泉涌般的文思，
文字尚未成为高高垒起的一堆书籍，
　如同谷仓尚未储藏饱满的成熟谷粒；
我翘首仰望，在星汉灿烂的夜空，
　大块云朵象征高尚浪漫传奇，
我又痛心想到，我不能幸运活着，
　用灵感的魔手描绘想象力的影子；
我感到，你，反复无常的美人！
　我将再也不能把你深情凝睇，
再也不能沉醉在豪放不羁的情感，
　体味爱的魅力——于是，我孤独伫立
在无边辽阔世界的岸边，冥想深思
直到爱情和名声沉入虚无之渊底。

Live in This

William Shakespeare (1564-1616)

Not marble nor the gilded monuments
Of princes, shall outlive this powerful rhyme,
But you shall shine more bright in these contents
Than unswept stone, besmeared with sluttish time.
When wasteful war shall statues overturn,
And broils root out the work of masonry,
Nor Mars his sword nor war's quick fire shall burn
The living record of your memory.
'Gainst death and all oblivious enmity
Shall you pace forth; your praise shall still find room
Even in the eyes of all posterity
That wear this world out to the ending doom.
So, till the judgement that yourself arise,
You live in this, and dwell in lovers' eyes.

活在诗中

[英] 威廉·莎士比亚

王公们的大理石或者镀金的纪念碑，
都不如这强有力的诗行不朽永垂，
比起时光弄污的没有清理的碑石，
你这些内容将闪耀更亮眼的光辉。
当毁灭一切的战争将雕像崩摧，
战火燃烧扫荡建筑物成为废墟，
战神刀剑或者战争烈焰都不会
将你记忆的活生生的历史烧毁。
对抗这死亡和湮灭一切的仇恨，
你自豪迈步；对你的赞美将长存，
甚至在千秋万代子孙的眼睛辉映，
哪怕直到这个世界耗尽末日来临。
　这样，直到最后审判你自己复苏，
　活在诗中，活在恋人的眼里。

That Time of Year Thou Mayst in Me Behold

William Shakespeare (1564-1616)

That time of year thou mayst in me behold
When yellow leaves, or none, or few, do hang
Upon those boughs which shake against the cold,
Bare ruined choirs, where late the sweet birds sang.
In me thou see'st the twilight of such day
As after sunset fadeth in the west;
Which by and by black night doth take away,
Death's second self, that seals up all in rest.
In me thou see'st the glowing of such fire
That on the ashes of his youth doth lie,
As the death-bed whereon it must expire,
Consumed with that which it was nourished by.
    This thou perceiv'st, which makes thy love more strong,
    To love that well which thou must leave ere long.

你可能在我身上看到这个时令

［英］威廉·莎士比亚

你可能在我身上看到这个时令
黄叶儿落地，或有几片叶儿飘荡，
迎着寒风在那光秃枝条上抖动，
歌坛荒废，可爱鸣禽曾在那歌唱。
在我身上你看见余生的暮霭
好像日落后在西天渐渐消逝，
不久以后，黑夜真的就要到来，
万物沉沉入睡，全都闭眼静息。
你看见我身上这样的火焰摇曳，
是在那青春的残留灰烬上燃烧，
正如在临终的床上它必须熄灭，
消耗殆尽所有滋养火头的燃料。
　你已经认知，你的爱就会更加强烈，
　好好爱我吧，不用多久你也将离去。

Elizabeth Barrett Browning (1806-1861)

How Do I Love Thee?

How do I love thee? Let me count the ways.
I love thee to the depth and breadth and height
My soul can reach, when feeling out of sight
For the ends of Being and ideal Grace,
I love thee to the level of every day's
Most quiet need, by sun and candlelight.
I love thee freely, as men strive for Right;
I love thee purely, as they turn from Praise.
I love thee with the passion put to use
In my old griefs, and with my childhood's faith.
I love thee with a love I seemed to lose
With my lost saints,—I love thee with the breath,
Smiles, tears, of all my life!—and, if God choose,
I shall but love thee better after death.

我该如何爱你?

［英］伊丽莎白·巴蕾特·勃朗宁

我该如何爱你？让我将各种方法细数。
我爱你，极尽我心灵能及的深挚、宽广和高远，
如同探求生命终极和神灵恩典
直到我的感觉视野外不能触及之处。
我爱你，借助着阳光和烛焰，
达到每天最恬静需要的程度。
我自由地爱你，像男子汉争取自身权利；
我纯洁地爱你，像他们对赞美予以回避。
我爱你，以我童真的诚意，满怀激情，
挥洒我往昔所有的辛酸苦涩。
我爱你，怀拥着我似乎因失去圣者
而消逝的爱慕之情，——我爱你，伴随呼吸、
微笑和泪水，以至整个生命！——如果上帝允许，
但愿死后，我仍然只会更诚挚地爱你。

Percy Bysshe Shelley (1792-1822)

To—

One word is too often profaned
For me to profane it,
One feeling too falsely disdained
For thee to disdain it;
One hope is too like despair
For prudence to smother,
And pity from thee more dear
Than that from another.

I can give not what men call love,
But wilt thou accept not
The worship the heart lifts above
And the Heavens reject not,—
The desire of the moth for the star,
Of the night for the morrow,
The devotion to something afar
From the sphere of our sorrow.

致——

[英]珀西·比希·雪莱

有一个词经常被人滥用
　我不会再来加以亵渎，
有一种感情错误地被人轻视
　你也不会再对此鄙薄；
有一种希望太过像绝望，
　即使谨慎也难免破碎，
但是来自你内心的怜悯
　应该比别人的更加珍贵。

我奉献的不是常言的爱情，
　而是我心底发出的敬仰，
即使上帝也不会拒绝——
　不知你愿不愿意珍赏？
仿佛飞蛾对星星的追求
　黑夜对黎明的企望，
这是我们悲苦的星球，
　对未来远景的热烈向往。

Stanzas for Music

George Gordon Byron (1788-1824)

There be none of Beauty's daughters
With a magic like thee;
And like music on the waters
Is thy sweet voice to me:
When, as if its sound were causing
The charmed Ocean's pausing,
The waves lie still and gleaming,
And the lull'd winds seem dreaming.

And the Midnight Moon is weaving
Her bright chain o'er the deep;
Whose breast is gently heaving,
As an infant's asleep:
So the spirit bows before thee,
To listen and adore thee;
With a full but soft emotion,
Like the swell of Summer's ocean.

为谱乐的诗章

[英]乔治·戈登·拜伦

没有一位美神的女儿，
如你这样魅力难当；
好像水面飘荡的音乐
送给我甜美的声浪：
仿佛这美妙乐音引起
海洋陶醉而停止跳荡，
波浪平静地闪烁微光，
风儿停息也进入梦乡。

午夜的月亮在深海处
编织她璀璨的项链；
大海乳房微微起伏，
好像一个沉睡婴孩：
这精灵在你前面俯身
静静倾听，对你崇拜；
怀着强烈而柔和的情感，
像夏天的海浪汹涌澎湃。

Shall I Compare Thee to a Summer's Day?

William Shakespeare (1564-1616)

Shall I compare thee to a summer's day?
Thou art more lovely and more temperate.
Rough winds do shake the darling buds of May,
And summer's lease hath all too short a date.
Sometime too hot the eye of heaven shines,
And often is his gold complexion dimmed,
And every fair from fair sometime declines,
By chance, or nature's changing course untrimm'd;
But thy eternal summer shall not fade
Nor lose possession of that fair thou ow'st[1],
Nor shall death brag thou wander'st in his shade
When in eternal lines to time thou grow'st.
So long as men can breathe, or eyes can see,
So long lives this, and this gives life to thee.

[1] 古英语中第二人称单数的谓语加 st 或 est.

我是否可以把你比作夏日？

[英] 威廉·莎士比亚

我是否可以把你比作夏日？
你可比夏天更可爱更温煦。
狂风摇落五月珍爱的花蕾，
夏天租借期限又过于短促。
有时苍天的眼睛闪耀热情光辉，
它那金色的面容经常也会阴晦；
世间每一种美丽终将会衰萎，
因机缘或天道变化面目全非。
但是你永久的夏天将不会消退，
你拥有的美丽也不会完全凋零；
死神不会夸说你在他阴影里徘徊，
你将在永恒的诗行里与时间永生：
　只要人们可以呼吸，眼睛可以注视，
　这首诗能够永存，并将生命赐予你。

The Presence of Love

Samuel Taylor Coleridge (1772-1834)

And in Life's noisiest hour,
There whispers still the ceaseless Love of Thee,
The heart's Self-solace and soliloquy.
You mould my Hopes, you fashion me within;
And to the leading Love-throb in the Heart
Thro' all my Being, thro' my pulses beat;
You lie in all my many Thoughts, like Light,
Like the fair light of Dawn, or summer Eve
On rippling Stream, or cloud-reflecting Lake.
And looking to the Heaven, that bends above you,
How oft! I bless the Lot, that made me love you.

爱的存在

[英]塞缪尔·泰勒·柯尔律治

在生活中最喧嚣的时刻，
依然在那里低语着对你永不休止的爱，
这个心灵的自慰和独白。
你铸造我的希望，你在内部塑造我；
直到引导我心中的爱的悸动
贯穿我的全部生命，贯穿我的脉搏跳动；
你展现在我的许多念头中，像光一样，
就像黎明的晨光，或是夏天傍晚的霞光
在潺潺的溪流上，或映射云朵的湖面上。
期待着苍天，俯身于你，
常年不断！我祝福所有人，让我永远爱你。

Life in a Love

Robert Browning (1812-1889)

Escape me?
Never—
Beloved!
While I am I, and you are you,
So long as the world contains us both,
Me the loving and you the loth,
While the one eludes, must the other pursue.
My life is a fault at last, I fear:
It seems too much like a fate, indeed!
Though I do my best I shall scarce succeed.

But what if I fail of my purpose here?
It is but to keep the nerves at strain,
To dry one's eyes and laugh at a fall,
And, baffled, get up to begin again—
So the chase takes up one's life, that's all.
While, look but once from your farthest bound
At me so deep in the dust and dark,
No sooner the old hope drops to ground
Than a new one, straight to the selfsame mark,
I shape me—
Ever
Removed!

爱的生活

[英] 罗伯特·勃朗宁

逃避我？
决不——
亲爱的！
虽然我是我，你是你，
只要世界包容我们两人，
我深爱钟情而你不愿意，
虽然一个是躲避，而另一个是穷追不舍。
我的生活最终是一个错误，我害怕：
它似乎太像一个天数，真的！
我也难于成功，尽管我竭尽全力。

但如果我达不到我的目的又有什么？
它只不过让我神经紧张保持到底，
擦干眼泪，跌了跤一笑置之，
挫败了，站起来重新开始——
这样的追逐付出一生，矢志不移。
虽然，你在最远地方才能回顾
我深陷在尘土和黑暗里，
一旦旧的希望跌落地上
新的希望，直接重新升起，
我要坚持——
永远
不会放弃！

To a Stranger

Walt Whitman (1819-1892)

Passing stranger! You do not know how longingly I look upon you,
You must be he I was seeking, or she I was seeking (it comes to me as a dream),
I have somewhere surely lived a life of joy with you,
All is recall'd as we flit by each other, fluid, affectionate, chaste, matured,
You grew up with me, were a boy with me or a girl with me,
I ate with you and slept with you, your body has become not yours only nor left my body mine only,
You give me the pleasure of your eyes, face, flesh as we pass, you take of my beard, breast, hands, in return,
I am not to speak to you, I am to think of you when I sit alone or wake at night alone,
I am to wait, I do not double I am to meet you again,
I am to see to it that I do not lose you.

致一个陌生人

［美］沃尔特·惠特曼

过路的陌生人哟！你不知道我是多么渴望见到你，

你一定是我正在追求的男人，或者一定是我正在追求的女人（来到我面前正如梦幻一般），

我肯定在某个地方曾与你一起度过快乐的生活，

当我们彼此擦身而过时一切都会回想起来，优雅的、爱慕的、贞洁的、成熟的，

你与我一起成长，曾经与我一起是个少男，或者，与我一起是个少女，

我与你一起吃饭、一起睡觉，你的身体变成不只是你的，我的身体剩下也不只是我的，

当我们一起度过时，你的眼睛、脸面、肉体给予我快乐，作为回报，你也从我的胡须、胸膛、双手得到快乐，

我没有对你说，当我独自坐着或夜间醒来，我想念你，独自一人

我等待着，我不怀疑，我一定会再遇见你

我会留意你，我不能错失你。

Chance

Chance says,
come here,
chance says,
can you bear

to part?
chance says,
sweetheart,
we haven't loved

for almost a year,
can you bear
this loneliness?
I can't;

apart from you,
I fear
wind,
bird,
sea

wave,
low places
and the high air;

I hear
dire threat
everywhere;
I start

at wind
in sycamores,
I can't bear
anything

further;
chance says,
dear,
I'm here,

don't you want me
any more?

缘分

[美]希尔达·杜利特尔

缘分说，
来到这里，
缘分说，
你能够忍受

分离吗？
缘分说，
甜心，
我们没有爱

几乎有一年了，
你能够忍受
这种孤独吗？
我不能；

与你分离，
我害怕
风，
鸟，
害怕大海，

波浪，
低洼的地方
和高空大气；

我听见
可怕威胁
无处不在；
我开始

在狂风中
在梧桐树林里，
我再往前
不能忍受

一切；
缘分说，
亲爱的，
我在这儿，

你现在不再
想要我了吗？

Christina Rossetti (1830-1894)

The First Day

I wish I could remember that first day,
First hour, first moment of your meeting me,
If bright or dim the season, it might be
Summer or Winter for aught I can say;
So unrecorded did it slip away,
So blind was I to see and to foresee,
So dull to mark the budding of my tree
That would not blossom for many a May.
If only I could recollect it, such
A day of days! I let it come and go
As traceless as a thaw of bygone snow;
It seemed to mean so little, meant so much;
If only now I could recall that touch,
First touch of hand in hand—Did one but know!

第一天

[英] 克里斯蒂娜·罗塞蒂

但愿我能够记得我遇见你的
第一天、第一个钟头、第一个时刻；
如果这个季节明朗或阴晦，它可能是
夏天或冬天，我也许只能如此说。
如此没有记录，它已悄悄溜过，
我看见和预见的都是茫然无知，
我是如此迟钝，我的树的花蕾
到五月了，许多已经错过花期。
但愿我一生中能够清楚记住
这样的一天！我就让它来来去去
如同往日的积雪融化毫无踪迹。
它意味深长，又似乎毫无意义！
那次触摸，如果现在我能够回忆，
第一次牵手的抚摸！——岂止是相识！

A Dedication to My Wife

Thomas Stearns Eliot (1888-1965)

To whom I owe the leaping delight
That quickens my senses in our waking time
And the rhythm that governs the repose of our sleeping time,
    The breathing in unison

Of loves whose bodies smell of each other
Who think the same thoughts without need of speech
And babble the same speech without need of meaning.

No peevish winter wind shall chill
No sullen tropic sun shall wither
The roses in the rose-garden which is ours and ours only

But this dedication is for others to read:
These are private words addressed to you in public.

献给我的妻子

[英] 托马斯·斯特尔那斯·艾略特

我应该给予你跳跃的喜悦
我们苏醒时分激活我的感官
加快这个支配我们睡眠时休息的心律，
　　这个呼吸合二为一

爱人们的身体散发彼此的气味
我们怀有同样的想法无须言语
喋喋不休着同样的话语没有含义。

没有凛冽冬风也会感到寒冷
没有灼人的烈日也会带来枯萎
这些我们专属玫瑰园盛开的玫瑰

但这个献诗给他人阅读：
这些对你说的悄悄话公之于众。

First Love

John Clare (1793-1864)

I ne'er was struck before that hour
With love so sudden and so sweet;
Her face it bloomed like a sweet flower
And stole my heart away complete.
My face turned pale as deadly pale,
My legs refused to walk away,
And when she looked what could I ail?
My life and all seemed turned to clay.

And then my blood rushed to my face
And took my sight away;
The trees and bushes found the place
Seemed midnight at noonday.
I could not see a single thing,
Words from my eyes did start;
They spoke as chords do from the string
And blood burnt round my heart.

Are flowers the winter's choice?

　　Is love's bed always snow?

She seemed to hear my silent voice,

　　Not love's appeal to know.

I never saw so sweet a face

　　As that I stood before:

My heart has left its dwelling-place

　　And can return no more.

John Clare (1793-1864)

初恋

爱情来得这样突然这样甜蜜，
　　在那个时刻前我从未曾激动。
她的美丽脸蛋像盛开的花朵，
　　完完全全掳走我的幼稚心魂。
我的脸变得苍白，死一般苍白，
　　可是我的双脚不愿挪动一步，
当她注视时我可能苦恼什么？
　　我的生命和一切都化为泥土。

那时我的血液涌上我的脸，
　　我的双眼移开，不能直视。
那个地方周围的树林和灌木
　　中午似乎像是半夜，迷茫宁谧。
我甚至看不见一样物体，
　　我的眼睛开始说出话语；
它们好像琴弦上的和弦，
　　血液在我的心脏周围沸腾。

鲜花是不是冬天的选择？
　　爱床上为何总是铺满冰雪？
她似乎听到我低声细语，
　　爱情的诉求没有得到理解。
我从未见过这么俏丽的容颜，
　　我纹丝不动在她面前静待：
我的心已经离开它原来居所
　　永远放飞，不可能再归来。

Amy Lowell (1874-1925)
［美］艾米·洛威尔

Decade

When you came , you were like red wine and honey,
And the taste of you burnt my mouth with its sweetness.
Now you are like morning bread,
Smooth and pleasant.
I hardly taste you at all for I know your savour,
But I am completely nourished.

十年间

刚来时，你那时喜欢红酒和蜂蜜，
你的味道燃烧我的嘴带有香甜味。
现在你喜欢早餐的面包，
可口而惬意。
我几乎完全不会品尝你，因为我熟悉你的滋味。
但是我完全接受你的滋养。

PRINCEZNA HYACINTA
Mucha

Mucha

Mucha

Mucha

SARAH·BERNHARDT
EN
L'HONNEUR
de
SARAH BERNHARDT
ses admirateurs et ses amis

Love's Memories

John Clare (1793-1864)

[英] 约翰·克莱尔

Love's memories haunt my footsteps still
　　Like ceaseless flowings of the river.
Its mystic depths say what can fill?
　　Sad disappointment waits forever.

爱情记忆

爱情记忆依然萦绕着我的脚步，
　　像这条河水永无休止地流淌。
什么可以填满它神秘的深度？
　　永远在等待伤心欲绝的失望。

One Day I Wrote Her Name upon the Strand

Edmund Spenser (1552-1599)

One day I wrote her name upon the strand,
But came the waves and washed it away:
Again I wrote it with a second hand,
But came the tide, and made my pains his prey.
"Vain man,"said she, "that dost in vain assay,
A mortal thing so to immortalize,
For I myself shall like to this decay,
And eke my name be wiped out likewise."
"Not so,"quod I, "let baser things devise
To die in dust, but you shall live by fame:
My verse your virtues rare shall eternize,
And in the heavens write your glorious name:
Where, whenas death shall all the world subdue,
Our love shall live, and later life renew."

有一天，我把她的名字写在海滩上

[英] 埃德蒙・斯宾塞

有一天，我把她的名字写在海滩上，
　但一波波海浪滚过把它冲去；
于是我又将她的名字重新写上，
　但潮水汹涌，把我的痛苦吞噬。
“自负的人，”她说，“这都是徒劳，
　如要终有一死的事物不朽一样；
因为我自己将会像这样终老，
　换上我的名字也同样会消亡。”
“不是这样，”我说，“让低贱者预想
　在尘土里死去，但你靠名声永生永世：
我的诗句使你的美德万代颂扬，
　并在天堂里写上你的光荣姓氏：
　　死神将征服全世界，而在那里，
　　我们爱情将长生，不久生命重新开始。”

斯宾塞创造了优美流畅的九行体。他的十四行诗集《爱情小唱》出版于1595年，被视为近代英国诗发展的起点。本诗说的是，美人能因诗人歌颂而不朽。

Thomas Campbell (1777-1844)

Freedom and Love

How delicious is the winning
Of a kiss at love's beginning,
When two mutual hearts are sighing
For the knot there's no untying!

Yet remember, 'midst our wooing,
Love has bliss, but Love has ruing;
Other smiles may make you fickle,
Tears for other charms may trickle.

Love he comes, and Love he tarries,
Just as fate or fancy carries;
Longest stays, when sorest chidden;
Laughs and flies, when press'd and bidden.

Bind the sea to slumber stilly,
Bind its odor to the lily,

Bind the aspen ne'er to quiver,
Then bind Love to last forever.

Love's a fire that needs renewal
Of fresh beauty for its fuel:
Love's wing moults when caged and captured,
Only free, he soars enraptured.

Can you keep the bee from ranging
Or the ringdove's neck from changing?
No! nor fetter'd Love from dying
In the knot there's no untying.

自由与爱情

在爱情伊始撷取一个蜜吻
是多么美好，多么兴奋，
两颗共同的心同时叹息，
因为没有解开这个情结！

要记住，我们相互追求时，
爱有狂喜，但也会有破灭；
他人的嬉笑可以使你犹豫，
为他人的魅力，泪水暗流啜泣。

爱他的来到，爱他的等待，
一切正如命运或幻想带来；
最恼人的责备有最长久的厮守；
恳求与和解同时乐以忘忧。

锁定大海，让它平静沉睡，
锁定百合，让它吐露芬芳，

锁定白杨，让它挺立昂扬，
锁定爱情，直到地久天长。

爱情是火，需要时时更新，
美丽鲜艳也要燃料增进：
鸟儿捕获入笼，爱的翅膀换羽，
一旦自由，就狂喜而翱翔千里。

你能否阻止蜜蜂漫游四方，
又能否防止斑鸠的脖颈变样？
不！没有束缚的爱也会死去，
在那个情结没有解开之际。

Robert Herrick (1591-1674)

To Virgins, to Make Much of Time

Gather ye rosebuds while ye may,
   Old Time is still a-flying:
And this same flower that smiles today,
   Tomorrow will be dying.

The glorious lamp of heaven, the Sun,
   The higher he's a-getting
The sooner will his race be run,
   And nearer he's to setting.

That age is best which is the first,
   When youth and blood are warmer;
But being spent, the worse, and worst
   Times, still succeed the former.

Then be not coy, but use your time;
   And while ye may, go marry:
For having lost but once your prime,
   You may for ever tarry.

致处女，珍惜韶华

［英］罗伯特·赫里克

你要及时采摘玫瑰花蕾，
　往昔时光一去不回：
今天的鲜花笑逐颜开，
　到明天都会变成尘埃。

太阳，天庭辉煌的明灯，
　他冉冉上升直到中庭
他的脚步也会越来越快，
　过了顶峰就会西沉。

青春岁月是人生的精华，
　热情洋溢而焕发容光；
韶华荒废，人生一败涂地
　抓紧时机就如愿以偿。

不要忸怩，不要错失良机；
　只要你中意，就喜结连理：
你的黄金时光一旦失去，
　就可能永远独身而失意。

You and I

Henry Alford (1810-1871)

My hand is lonely for your clasping, dear;
  My ear is tired waiting for your call.
I want your strength to help, your laugh to cheer;
  Heart, soul and senses need you, one and all.
I droop without your full, frank sympathy;
  We ought to be together—you and I;
We want each other so, to comprehend
  The dream, the hope, things planned, or seen, or wrought.
Companion, comforter and guide and friend,
  As much as love asks love, does thought ask thought.
Life is so short, so fast the lone hours fly,
  We ought to be together, you and I.

你和我

［英］亨利·阿福德

我的手单单是为了给你握住，亲爱的，
　我的耳朵不辞疲累地等待着你的呼唤。
我想要你的力量帮助，你的微笑鼓舞；
　心、心灵和心智都需要你，全在期盼。
没有你充分慷慨的同情我将萎靡不振；
　我们应该在一起——你和我；
我们需要彼此这样，相互理解，
　一起梦想、希望、规划、聚会或者工作。
我们是同伴、安慰者、指引者和朋友，
　正如爱祈求爱，思慕招引思慕。
生命这么短促，让孤单时刻快快飞逝，
　我们应该永远在一起，你和我。

Solo for Saturday Night Guitar

Carl Sandburg (1878-1967)

Time was. Time is. Time shall be.
Man invented time to be used.
Love was. Love is. Love shall be.
Yet man never invented love
Nor is love to be used like time.
A clock wears numbers one to twelve
And you look and read its face
And tell the time pre-cise-ly ex-act-ly.
Yet who reads the face of love?
Who tells love numbers pre-cise-ly ex-act-ly?
Holding love in a tight hold for keeps,
Fastening love down and saying
"It's here now and here for always."
You don't do this offhand, careless-like.
Love costs. Love is not so easy
Nor is the shimmering of star dust
Nor the smooth flow of new blossoms

Nor the drag of a heavy hungering for someone.
Love is a white horse you ride
or wheels and hammers leaving you lonely
or a rock in the moonlight for rest
or a sea where phantom ships cross always
or a tall shadow always whispering
or a circle of spray and prisms—
maybe a rainbow round your shoulder.
Heavy heavy is love to carry
and light as one rose petal,
light as a bubble, a blossom,
a remembering bar of music
or a finger or a wisp of hair
never forgotten.

Carl Sandburg (1878-1967)

周六晚上吉他独奏

时间永远不停地流逝。
人类发明利用时间。
爱永远不断地衍生。
人类还从未发明过爱，
爱也不像时间被利用。
钟呈现数字从一到十二，
你注视和阅读它的钟面
精确而准确地说出时间。
又有谁能读出爱的钟面？
谁能精确而准确地告诉爱的数字？
握着爱紧握着保持爱，
锁定爱并说着
“现在爱在这里，永远在这里。”
你不要这么随意，漫不经心。
爱需要付出代价。爱不是这么轻易，
也不像星尘闪烁光芒，

也不是初开的花朵竞相绽放，
也不是热烈而吃力地追求某人。
爱是你骑的一匹白马
或是让你孤单的轮子和锤子
或是月光下休息的一块岩石
或是幽灵船永远跨越的大海
或是总是窃窃私语的高高阴影
或是一圈圈喷雾和棱镜——
也许是你肩膀上的彩虹。
携带着沉甸甸的爱
和像一朵玫瑰花瓣的光，
像一个泡沫、一朵花的光，
一间难忘的音乐酒吧
或是一根手指或一绺头发
决不会忘记。

Anne Bronte (1820-1849)

Appeal

Oh, I am very weary,
Though tears no longer flow;
My eyes are tired of weeping,
My heart is sick of woe;

My life is very lonely
My days pass heavily,
I'm weary of repining;
Wilt thou not come to me?

Oh, didst thou know my longings
For thee, from day to day,
My hopes, so often blighted,
Thou wouldst not thus delay!

诉求

[英]安妮·勃朗特

啊，我已经心灰意懒，
尽管我已经不再流泪；
我的眼睛早已厌倦哭泣，
我的心正在忍痛含悲；

我的生活孤苦无依，
我的日子度日如年，
我厌倦怨天尤人；
你难道不来找我吗？

啊，你知道我在期盼
为了你，一天又一天，
我的希望，经常落空，
请你不要这样拖延！

Ruth

Thomas Hood (1799-1845)

She stood breast high amid the corn,
Clasped by the golden light of morn,
Like the sweetheart of the sun,
Who many a glowing kiss had won.

On her cheek an autumn flush,
Deeply ripened; such a blush
In the midst of brown was born,
Like red poppies grown with corn.

Round her eyes her tresses fell,
Which were blackest none could tell,
But long lashes veiled a light,
That had else been all too bright.

And her hat, with shady brim,
Made her tressy forehead dim—

Thus she stood amid the stooks,
Praising God with sweetest looks:

Sure, I said, heaven did not mean,
Where I reap thou shouldst but glean,
Lay they sheaf adown and come,
Share my harvest and my home.

露丝

Thomas Hood (1799-1845)

她高挺胸脯站在玉米地，
早晨金色霞光披拂全身，
宛如是太阳的心上人，
赢得许多次灼热的亲吻。

她的脸颊透露深秋的红晕，
成熟的色调；这样的赧颜，
在生成的棕褐色皮肤中间，
像红罂粟夹在玉米地里面。

她的长发垂落在她眼睛旁，
没有人能说清楚哪个最黑俏，
但长睫毛掩饰一丝光亮，
眼珠不会显得过于闪耀。

她的帽子投下阴暗的边缘，
隐约可见一绺头发和额际——

她就这样站在麦草垛中间，
以最甜美的笑颜赞扬上帝：

当然，我说，上天没有此意，
我将收获你而不是拾落麦穗，
将麦草捆扎起来放下，过来吧，
分享我的收成和我的住所。

Red and White Roses

Thomas Carew (1595-1640)

Read in these Roses the sad story
Of my hard fate, and your owne glory.
In the White you may discover
The paleness of a fainting lover;
In the Red the flames still feeding
On my heart, with fresh wounds bleeding.
The White will tell you how I languish,
And the Red express my anguish;
The White my innocence displaying,
The Red my martyrdom betraying.
The frowns that on your brow resided,
Have those Roses thus divided.
Oh! Let your smiles but clear the weather,
And then they both shall grow together.

红玫瑰和白玫瑰

[英] 托马斯·卡鲁

阅读这些玫瑰里的悲伤故事——
我的难解命运，还有你的荣耀福气。
在白玫瑰中，你可以发现
心神不定的爱人脸色苍白；
在红玫瑰中，我心上的火焰
依然燃烧，新的创伤在出血。
白玫瑰告诉你，我的心备受折磨，
而红玫瑰则表达我的极度痛楚；
白玫瑰展示我的纯洁忠诚，
红玫瑰显露我的献身牺牲。
在你的额头上一直愁眉不展，
这些玫瑰就这样交相争妍。
啊！但愿你的微笑像天气晴朗，
让这双色玫瑰一起生长开放。

William Butler Yeats (1865-1939)

Never Give All the Heart

Never give all the heart, for love
Will hardly seem worth thinking of
To passionate women, if it seem
Certain, and they never dream
That it fades out from kiss to kiss;
For everything that's lovely is
But a brief dreamy kind delight.
O never give the heart outright
For they, for all smooth lips can say,
Have given their hearts up to the play.
And who could play it well enough
If deaf and dumb and blind with love?
He that made this knows all the cost
For he gave all his heart and lost.

决不要全抛一片心

[爱尔兰] 威廉·巴特勒·叶芝

为爱情不要全抛一片心，
不值得考虑放荡的女人，
这感情未必是一心一意，
她们决不追求梦想成真，
爱早已从一次次亲吻中消逝；
一切所谓的美好和可爱
不过是短暂的梦幻欢喜。
哦，决不要彻底抛却一片心，
因为她们习惯于油嘴滑舌，
已经将心思全付诸这个游戏。
如果因爱成为又聋又哑又盲，
谁能得心应手玩得称心如意？
他这样做已经知道所有成本，
因为他把心全抛出无法挽回。

Thomas Hardy (1840-1928)

Thunderstorm in Town

A reminiscence: 1893

She wore a new "terra-cotta" dress,
And we stayed, because of the pelting storm,
Within the hansom's dry recess,
Though the horse had stopped; yea, motionless
    We sat on, snug and warm.

Then the downpour ceased, to my sharp sad pain,
And the glass that had screened our forms before
Flew up, and out she sprang to her door:
I should have kissed her if the rain
    Had lasted a minute more.

小城暴雨
（1893年一件往事）

[英] 托马斯·哈代

她穿了件赤褐色的新衣服，
因为滂沱大雨，我们逗留，
在双座小马车的干燥车厢里，
尽管辕马站住；嗯，一动不动，
　　我们偎坐着，温暖而舒适。

倾盆大雨骤停，我钻心的悲痛，
之前这玻璃掩饰我们的形体，
突然打开，她跳出去奔到门口：
我应该亲吻她，假如这雨
　　再持续多下一分钟。

哈代以小说《德伯家的苔丝》等闻名。但他文学生涯的初期和晚期与诗歌创作密不可分。这首诗，展示了作者因为笨拙而错失一个爱情的机会，导致其长期遗憾。哈代以厌世主义著称，这段往事轻描淡写地展现出了他的另一面。

I Carry Your Heart with Me

E.E.Cummings (1894-1962)

i[1] carry your heart with me(i carry it in my heart)
i am never without it(anywhere
i go you go, my dear; and whatever is done
by only me is your doing, my darling)
                                        i fear
no fate (for you are my fate, my sweet) i want
no world (for beautiful you are my world, my true)
and it's you are whatever a moon has always meant
and whatever a sun will always sing is you

here is the deepest secret nobody knows
(here is the root of the root and the bud of the bud
and the sky of the sky of a tree called life; which grows
higher than soul can hope or mind can hide)
and this is the wonder that's keeping the stars apart

i carry your heart (i carry it in my heart).

[1] 第一人称小写“i”是肯明斯诗歌的独特的排字法。

我将你的心带在身上

[美] E.E. 肯明斯

我将你的心带在身上（我把它放在我的心里珍藏），
我从未离开过它（无论我去哪里，都有你陪伴在我身旁，
我的宝贝；无论我做什么哪怕是我孤军奋战，都有你给我力量，我亲爱的），

我害怕；

不是命运（因为你就是我的命运，我的爱人），我想要的
不是整个世界（因为你的美丽就是我的世界，我的真爱），
正是有了你，无论如何月亮才有意义，
无论如何太阳将永远歌唱的是你；

这里最深奥的秘密没有人知道
（这里是根之根、蓓蕾之蓓蕾、天空之天空、一棵树称之为生命；这棵树生长远远高于心灵所期望或头脑所隐藏），
这是奇迹，足以使星星分隔两地。

我将你的心带在身上（我把它放在我的心里珍藏）。

Song to Celia

Ben Jonson (1572-1637)

Drink to me, only, with thine eyes,
And I will pledge with mine;
Or leave a kiss but in the cup,
And I'll not look for wine;
The thirst that from the soul doth rise,
Doth ask a drink divine:
But might I of Jove's nectar sup,
I would not change for thine.

I sent thee late a rosy wreath,
Not so much honoring thee,
As giving it a hope, that there
It could not wither'd be;
But thou thereon did'st only breathe;
And sent'st it back to me:
Since when it grows, and smells, I swear,
Not of itself, but thee.

致西莉亚的歌

［英］本·琼生

你只用美目与我干杯，
我用我深情眼神同酬；
你只留下一个吻在杯中，
我今后不再寻觅美酒。
这从内心深处升腾的渴望，
来要求这神圣的一口：
哪怕有人给我天帝琼浆，
因为你，我不会与之换酒。

我刚刚送给你玫瑰花环，
表示我对你爱慕无比，
因为我寄托一个希望，
花儿在你身旁永不枯萎。
但只要你吸进花的芬芳，
就会向我呼出更多香气；
我确信，花儿依然生长飘香，
馨香的不是花，而是因为你。

琼生是莎士比亚同时代人，其名气与莎翁不相上下。这首诗是著名情歌，是传世之作，写得典雅别致，早已被谱成歌曲，传唱至今。

Amy Lowell (1874-1925)

Vernal Equinox

The scent of hyacinths, like a pale mist,
lies between me and my book;
And the South Wind, washing through the room,
Makes the candles quiver.
My nerves sting at a spatter of rain on the shutter,
And I am uneasy with the thrusting of green shoots
Outside, in the night.

Why are you not here to overpower me with your tense and
urgent love?

春分

[美] 艾米·洛威尔

风信子的香味，像一片白雾，散发在我与我的书之间；

这阵南风，冲洗进这些房间，
让烛光摇曳不定。
我的神经感到剧痛，雨水飞溅在百叶窗上，
我心神不安，因为绿色的新芽在伸展
在户外，在夜晚。

你为什么不在这里，以你的紧张和迫切的爱深深感动我？

Robert Burns (1759-1796)

A Red, Red Rose

O my luve's like a red, red rose,
That's newly sprung in June;
O my luve's like the melodie,
That's sweetly played in tune.

As fair art thou, my bonnie lass,
So deep in luve am I;
And I will love thee still, my dear,
Till a' the seas gang dry.

Till a' the seas gang dry, my dear,
And the rocks melt wi' the sun:
O I will love thee still, my dear,
While the sands o' life shall run.

And fare thee weel, my only luve,
And fare thee weel a while!
And I will come again, my luve,
Though it were ten thousand mile!

一朵红红的玫瑰

［英］罗伯特·彭斯

啊，我的爱人像朵红红的玫瑰，
在六月里簇新地绽放；
啊！我的爱人像这支动听乐曲，
演奏的旋律美妙悠扬。

你这么可爱，我美丽的姑娘，
我爱着你，情深似壑，
我将永远爱你，我亲爱的，
直到汪洋大海干涸。

直到汪洋大海干涸，我亲爱的，
直到太阳能将岩石化融；
啊！我将依然爱你，我亲爱的，
只要生命之沙还会流动。

我要与你告别，我唯一的爱人，
我将与你告别一会儿！
我定将再次回来，我的爱人，
哪怕它相隔千里万里。

Edgar Allan Poe (1809-1849)

To Helen

Helen, thy beauty is to me
　Like those Nicean barks of yore,
That gently, o'er a perfumed sea,
　The weary, way-worn wanderer bore
　To his own native shore.

On desperate seas long wont to roam,
　Thy hyacinth hair, thy classic face,
Thy Naiad airs have brought me home
　To the glory that was Greece,
　And the grandeur that was Rome.

Lo! in yon brilliant window-niche
　How statue-like I see thee stand,

The agate lamp within thy hand!
　Ah, Psyche, from the regions which
　Are Holy-Land!

致海伦

海伦，我看你的美丽，
　如同往昔尼西亚的三桅船，
载着疲倦的、流落异乡的游子
　悠然地航行在芳香馥郁的海洋，
　回归他故乡的海岸。

在惊涛骇浪在海洋上浪迹天涯，
　你飘逸秀发，你典雅脸庞，
你那奈达仙女的风采引导我抵家
　达到古希腊的荣耀，
　达到古罗马的辉煌。

看！在那明亮的窗户壁龛上
　我看见你雕塑般站立，

你的手里还握有玛瑙灯！
　啊，你是赛姬，你来自天国
　神圣的土地！

在这古典主义的精致浪漫的再现中，爱伦·坡将强烈的节奏和重复的韵律柔软化。这首诗是从远方观看，几乎是祈祷般的崇拜心爱的人。海伦是希腊神话中宙斯之女。据称，灵感来自于同学母亲简·施坦纳太太（Mrs. Jane Stanard）。显然，她很仁慈亲切，鼓励他写作。诗中将她与神话中美丽的海伦类比。

Elizabeth Akers Allen (1832-1911)

At Last

At last, when all the summer shine
  That warmed life's early hours is past,
Your loving fingers seek for mine
  And hold them close—at last—at last!
Not oft the robin comes to build
  Its nest upon the leafless bough
By autumn robbed, by winter chilled —
  But you, dear heart, you love me now.

Though there are shadows on my brow
  And furrows on my cheek, in truth —
The marks where Time's remorseless plough
  Broke up the blooming sward of Youth —
Though fled is every girlish grace
  Might win or hold a lover's vow,
Despite my sad and faded face,
  And darkened heart, you love me now!

I count no more my wasted tears;
    They left no echo of their fall;
I mourn no more my lonesome years;
    This blessed hour atones for all.
I fear not all that Time or Fate
    May bring to burden heart or brow —
Strong in the love that came so late,
Our souls shall keep it always now!

Elizabeth Akers Allen (1832-1911)

终于

终于，整个夏季日子闪闪发光，
　那温暖人生的凌晨时分已经过去，
你抚爱的手指寻找我的手指
　紧紧握住——终于——终于紧握！
知更鸟不是经常地回来，
　在这无叶的树枝上筑窝，
到秋天被剥夺，到冬天就挨冻——
　但是你，亲爱的心，你现在爱我。

尽管我的眉头上有一片阴影
　我的脸颊上起了条条皱纹，事实是——
这些标志时间无情地耙犁
　结束了青春盛开花朵的草地——
尽管每一个少女的优雅消逝
　可以赢得或把握情人的海誓，
不管我的悲哀和褪色的脸庞，
　还有黯淡的心，你现在爱我！

我再也不计算我浪费的眼泪；

　它们落下也没有赚取回音；

我不再哀叹我孤寂的岁月；

　这祝福的时刻为所有人庆幸。

我完全不会担忧时机或命运

　可以压下心头的重担千钧——

爱情强大，虽然来得这么迟，

现在我们的心灵将其永远保存！

时机就是一切，特别是关于内心问题。这首诗谈论一个递延的恋情。两个情人最后在他们晚年的结合，他们的爱情最终要比以前曾经拥有的更强大，因为他们的感情经过了时间的考验。

Beauty That Is Never Old

James Weldon Johnson (1871-1938)

When buffeted and beaten by life's storms,
When by bitter cares of life oppressed,
I want no surer haven than your arms,
I want no sweeter heaven than your breast.

When over my life's way there falls the blight
Of sunless days, and nights of starless skies;
Enough for me, the calm and steadfast light
That softly shines within your loving eyes.

The world, for me, and all the world can hold
Is circled by your arms; for me there lies,
Within the lights and shadows of your eyes,
The only beauty that is never old.

永远不会衰老的美丽

［美］詹姆斯·韦尔登·约翰逊

当被生活的风暴折磨和打击，
当被生活的痛苦的忧虑压抑，
我想要避风港，数你的手臂更可靠，
我想要天堂，数你的胸膛更甜蜜。

我生活的道路上有时会降临灾祸
无阳光的日子和无星星的天幕，
只要你爱恋的眼睛里温柔地闪耀
平静而坚毅的光芒，我就心满意足。

这个世界，对于我而言，你的双臂
可以包围全世界；对于我，躺在这里，
在你的眼睛的光芒和阴影中，
永远不会衰老的只有这美丽。

John Wilmot (1648-1680)

To His Mistress

Why dost thou shade thy lovely face? O why
Does that eclipsing hand of thine deny
The sunshine of the Sun's enlivening eye?

Without thy light what light remains in me?
Thou art my life; my way, my light's in thee;
I live, I move, and by thy beams I see.

Thou art my life—if thou but turn away
My life's a thousand deaths. Thou art my way—
Without thee, Love, I travel not but stray.

My light thou art—without thy glorious sight
My eyes are darken'd with eternal night.
My Love, thou art my way, my life, my light.

致他的情人

[英] 约翰·威尔莫特

为什么你要掩盖你可爱的脸？哦，为什么
你这苍白失色的手拒绝分享
太阳生气勃勃的眼睛熠熠亮光？

没有你的光，有什么光留在我身上？
你是我的生命；我的方向、我的光明在你身上；
我生活，我活动，依靠我看见的你的光芒。

你是我的生命——如果你只要避开
我的生命有一千个死亡。你是我的方向——
没有你，亲爱的，我无法远行只能流浪。

你是我的光——没有你辉煌的景象
我的眼睛因永久的夜晚而黯然失神。
我的爱人，你是我的方向，我的生命，我的光明。

作者作为国王查理二世法院的风流才子而闻名，是著名的浪荡子。罗切斯特伯爵在这里巧妙地玩文字游戏，以太阳光与他的爱情之光、他的生命之光相类比。

The Passionate Shepherd to His Love

Christopher Marlowe (1564-1593)

Come live with me and be my love,
And we will all the pleasure prove
That valleys, groves, hills and fields,
Or woods or steepy mountain yields.

And we will sit upon the rocks,
And see the shepherds feed their flocks
By shallow rivers, to whose falls
Melodious birds sing madrigals.

And I will make thee beds of roses
And a thousand fragrant posies;
A cap of flowers, and a kirtle
Embroidered all with leaves of myrtle.

A gown made of the finest wool
Which from our pretty lambs we pull;

Fair lined slippers for the cold,
With buckles of the purest gold.

A belt of straw and ivy-buds
With coral clasps and amber studs:
And if these pleasures may thee move,
Come and live with me and be my love.

Thy shepherd swains shall dance and sing
For thy delight each May morning:
If these delights thy mind may move,
Then live with me and be my love.

激情牧羊人致他的爱人

Christopher Marlowe (1564-1593)

来吧，与我同居，做我的爱人
我们将体验所有的赏心乐事，
在这莽莽山谷、丛林、丘陵和田野，
还有林地或高山峻岭一同嬉戏。

我们将一起盘坐在岩石上，
遥望着牧羊人将羊群牧放，
在清浅的溪流边瀑布飞溅，
鸟儿歌声悦耳，婉转而悠扬。

我将为你定制玫瑰花床，
有一千束花朵散发芬芳；
戴一顶花帽，穿一袭长裙
桃金娘的树叶绣满裙上。

用最好的羊毛缝制长袍，

亲手剪自可爱的小羊羔；
做双有衬里的软鞋御寒，
精致的鞋扣用纯金打造。

麦草、常春藤叶芽编织腰带，
珊瑚做扣钩，琥珀做饰钉，
如果这些乐事可以打动你，
来吧，与我同居，做我的爱人。

每当五月清晨讨你的欢心，
你的牧羊人情郎歌舞尽兴：
如果这些欢乐能打动你心，
就与我同居，做我的爱人。

运用牧歌形式，以田园大自然作为背景，语言简洁朴实，表现牧羊人的大胆求情，直抒胸臆：跟我一起生活，做我的爱人。此诗广为传诵，并有众多应和者。

She Comes Not When Noon Is on the Roses

Herbert Trench (1865-1923)

She comes not when Noon is on the roses—
    Too bright is Day.
She comes not to Soul till it reposes
    From work and play.

But when Night is on the hills, and the great Voices
    Roll in from Sea.
By starlight and by candlelight and dreamlight
    She comes to me.

她没有来，正当中午玫瑰盛开时

［爱尔兰］赫伯特·特伦奇

她没有来，正当中午玫瑰盛开时——
　　白天太过绚丽。
她没有来，心灵仍然沉湎于
　　工作和游戏。

但当夜晚在山上，巨大的声浪
　　汹涌澎湃来自海洋，
借助星光、烛光和梦幻之光
　　她来到我的身旁。

这种爱情不是对一切人适用。特伦奇描写的爱情对于占有物质世界是太微妙，过于清丽脱俗。他的爱的对象出现像梦一样，因此仍然是高雅纯粹的。

Frank Dempster Sherman (1860-1916)

Love's Springtide

My heart was winter-bound until
I heard you sing;
O voice of Love, hush not, but fill
My life with Spring!

My hopes were homeless things before
I saw your eyes;
O smile of Love, close not the door
To paradise!

My dreams were bitter once, and then
I found them bliss;
O lips of Love, give me again
Your rose to kiss!

Springtide of love! The secret sweet
Is ours alone;
O heart of Love, at last you beat
Against my own!

爱之春潮

［美］弗兰克·邓普思特·谢尔曼

我的心一直被寒冬围困，
　直到我听见你唱歌；
哦，爱的声音，嘘，不作声，
　我的生活春光明媚！

我的希望曾经无家可归，
　在我看见你眼神以前；
哦，爱的微笑，不要将
　通往天堂门紧闭！

我的梦境一度痛苦万状，
　我现在发现是极乐天庭；
哦，爱的嘴唇，再一次给我
　你的玫瑰香吻！

爱之春潮啊！隐秘而甜美
　单独属于我们；
哦，爱的心，你的跳动终于
　紧贴我自己的心！

Love in Autumn

I sought among the drifting leaves,
The golden leaves that once were green,
To see if Love were hiding there
And peeping out between.

For thro' the silver showers of May
And thro' the summer's heavy heat,
In vain I sought his golden head
And light, fast-flying feet.

Perhaps when all the world is bare
And cruel winter holds the land,
The Love that finds no place to hide
Will run and catch my hand.

I shall not care to have him then,
I shall be bitter and a-cold—

It grows too late for frolicking
    When all the world is old.

The little hiding Love, come forth,
    Come forth before the autumn goes,
And let us seek thro' ruined paths
    The garden's last red rose.

Sara Teasdale (1884-1933)

秋天的爱

我在正在飘落的树叶中翻捡，
　　曾经翠绿的黄金色的叶片，
看看是否爱神躲藏在那里，
　　从落叶之间往外张望顾盼。

透过五月的银色的微微细雨，
　　透过夏天的烈日炎炎酷暑，
我徒然寻找他的金色的头颅
　　和轻盈的飞快行走的脚步。

也许当整个世界万物萧条，
　　朔风呼啸的冬天地冻天寒，
爱神发现没有地方躲风避寒，
　　将会跑过来紧抓我的手取暖。

到那时我将再不会关心他，
　　我将会强忍痛苦而冷眼相待——

所有的寻欢作乐都为时已晚，

　　全世界都显得龙钟老态。

小小的隐藏的爱神，快点出来吧，

　　一定要在秋天来临之前出来，

让我们通过荒废的小路去追寻，

　　花园里最后的一朵红玫瑰。

Thomas Moore (1779-1852)

The Monopolist

If I were yonder wave, my dear,
And thou the isle it clasps around,
I would not let a foot come near
My land of bliss, my fairy ground!

If I were yonder conch of gold,
And thou the pearl within it placed,
I would not an eye behold
The sacred gem my arm my arms embraced!

If I were yonder orange tree,
And thou the blossom blooming there,
I would not yield a breath of thee,
To scent the most imploring air!

独占者

[爱尔兰]托马斯·穆尔

如果我是那遥远的波浪，亲爱的，
你一定是它紧紧地搂拥的岛屿，
我不会容忍另一只脚走近，
我的极乐王国，我的仙女圣地！

如果我是那遥远的金色贝壳，
你就是安放其中的纯色珍珠，
我不会容忍一只眼暗中窥视，
我的双臂拥抱的神圣的宝石！

如果我是那远方的橙树，
你就是那里盛开的花朵，
我不会放弃你清香的呼吸，
我要深吸最沁人心脾的空气！

When I Heard at the Close of the Day

Walt Whitman (1819-1892)

When I heard at the close of the day how my name had been
receiv'd with plaudits in the capitol, still it was not a happy
night for me that follow'd,
And else when I carous'd, or when my plans were accomplish'd,
stilli was not happy,
But the day when I rose at dawn from the bed of perfect health,
refresh'd, singing, inhaling the ripe breath of autumn,
When I saw the full moon in the west grow pale and disappear
in the morning light,
When I wander'd alone over the beach, and undressing bathed,
laughing with the cool waters, and saw the sun rise,
And when I thought how my dear friend my lover was on his
way coming, O then I was happy,
O then each breath tasted sweeter, and all that day my food
nourish'd me more, and the beautiful day pass'd well,
And the next came with equal joy, and with the next at evening
came my friend,

And that night while all was still I heard the waters roll slowly continually up the shores,
I heard the hissing rustle of the liquid and sands as directed to me whispering to congratulate me,
For the one I love most lay sleeping by me under the same cover in the cool night,
In the stillness in the autumn moonbeams his face was inclined toward me,
And his arm lay lightly around my breast—and that night I was happy.

傍晚时分我听见

傍晚时分我听见我的名字在议会大厅接受掌声雷动，在当夜我仍然感受不到快乐，
当我欢宴，或当我的规划已经实现，我仍然感受不到快乐，
但那一天黎明我从床上起身拥有完美体魄，精力充沛，唱着歌，呼吸秋天成熟的气息，
当我看见西边的满月变白，消失在晨光中，
当我独自在海滩漫步，脱下衣服沐浴，与清凉的海水一起说笑，注视着太阳升起，
当我想着我亲爱的朋友、我的爱人正在来的路上，啊，那时我感到快乐，
啊，那时每一次呼吸都有更甜美的味道，那天我的所有食物都更滋养我，美丽的一天过得多美好，

第二天是同样的快乐，第二天夜晚我的朋友来到，
那晚万籁俱寂我仍然听到海水连绵不断地慢慢地滚上海滩，
我听见流水和沙粒在丝丝沙沙作响，对着我低语祝贺我，
因为我最爱的人躺着睡在我身旁在寒冷的夜晚在这同一张被子下，
在秋天月光下在寂静里他的脸俯向我，
他的手臂轻轻地围绕在我的胸膛——那一夜我很快乐。

William Blake (1757-1827)

[英] 威廉·布莱克

The Lily

The modest Rose puts forth a thorn,
The humble sheep a threat'ning horn;
While the Lily white shall in love delight,
Nor a thorn nor a threat stain her beauty bright.

百合花

羞怯的玫瑰长出尖刺，
谦恭的羊有威吓的角，
白色百合享受爱之快乐，
没有刺没有角使她更美丽。

Mucha

Mucha

Mucha

Mucha

Mucha

Mucha

SALON DES CENT
Juin 1897
31 rue Bonaparte
Exposition de l'Œuvre
de
A. MUCHA
IMP. F. CHAMPENOIS. PARIS.
Mucha

D. H. Lawrence (1885-1930)

［英］D.H. 劳伦斯

Green

The dawn was apple-green,
　The sky was green wine held up in the sun,
The moon was a golden petal between.

She opened her eyes, and green
　They shone, clear like flowers undone
For the first time, now for the first time seen.

绿

曙光是苹果绿，
　天空是阳光下举起的绿酒，
月亮是其中的金色花瓣。

她睁开眼睛，闪耀着
　绿色，清澈如第一次开放的花朵，
现在第一次显露。

I Love Thee

Thomas Hood (1799-1845)

I love thee—I love thee!
  'Tis all that I can say;
It is my vision in the night,
  My dreaming in the day;
The very echo of my heart,
  The blessing when I pray.
I love thee—I love thee!

I love thee—I love thee!
  Is ever on my tongue.
In all my proudest poesy
  That chorus still is sung;
It is the verdict of my eyes
  Amidst the gay and young:
I love thee—I love thee!
  A thousand maids among.

I love thee—I love thee!

  Thy bright and hazel glance,

The mellow lute upon those lips,

  Whose tender tones entrance.

But most dear heart of hearts, thy proofs.

  That still these words enhance!

I love thee—I love thee!

  Whatever be thy chance.

Thomas Hood (1799-1845)

我爱你

我爱你——我爱你！
　这句话胜过千言万语；
它是我在夜晚的幻象，
　是我在白日的梦呓；
它是我心跳的回声，
　是我祈祷的希冀。
我爱你——我爱你！

我爱你——我爱你！
　永远挂在我的唇舌。
在我最自豪的诗歌里
　那首歌依然在唱起；
它是我双眼的见证
　同伴和年轻人的交际：
我爱你——我爱你！
　你可是千里挑一。

我爱你——我爱你！
　你明亮和淡褐色一瞥，
那些唇上圆润的琴声，
　吐露出委婉的音律。
最亲爱的心上人啊，你的验证。
　依然增强这些话语！
我爱你——我爱你！
　无论如何都是你的机遇。

To My Dear and Loving Husband

Anne Bradstreet (1612-1672)

If ever two were one then surely we.
If ever man were loved by wife, than thee;
If ever wife were happy in a man,
Compare with me, ye women, if you can.
I prize thy love more than whole mines of gold
Or all the riches that the East doth hold.
My love is such that rivers cannot quench,
Nor aught but love from thee give recompense,
Thy love is such I can no way repay;
The heavens reward thee manifold, I pray.
Then while we live, in love let's so persevere
That when we live no more, we may live ever.

献给我亲爱的和挚爱的丈夫

如果真的有两个人可以合为一人，那就是我们。
如果真的有个男人被妻子疼爱，那就是你；
如果真的有妻子将终身幸福托付一个男人，
如果你可以，女士们，同我比一比。
我珍视你的爱胜过整座金矿，
也胜过东方所拥有的全部宝藏。
我的爱情如同这条河水长流不断，
只要你的爱，我不求任何报偿。
你的爱如此深沉，我无法回报。
我祈祷，上天给予你丰厚的奖赏。
我们活着，相亲相爱，让我们至死不渝，
直至我们不再生活，我们也可一如既往。

安妮与她丈夫于1628年结婚。后来他们从英国移居北美。她的诗集在1650年第一次出版。当时是相当秘密地带回英国印刷出版——在她不知情的情况下。

In the Gold Room: a Harmony

Oscar Wilde (1854-1900)

Her ivory hands on the ivory keys
   Strayed in a fitful fantasy,
Like the silver gleam when the poplar trees
   Rustle their pale leaves listlessly,
Or the drifting foam of a restless sea
When the waves show their teeth in the flying breeze.

Her gold hair fell on the wall of gold
   Like the delicate gossamer tangles spun
On the burnished disk of the marigold,
   Or the sun-flower turning to meet the sun
   When the gloom of the jealous night is done,
And the spear of the lily is aureoled.

And her sweet red lips on these lips of mine
   Burned like the ruby fire set
In the swinging lamp of a crimson shrine,
   Or the bleeding wounds of the pomegranate,
   Or the heart of the lotus drenched and wet
With the split-out blood of the rose-red wine.

在金色的房间：一种和谐

[英] 奥斯卡·王尔德

她象牙色的双手在象牙色的键盘上，
　　以一种断断续续的幻想随意弹响，
像白杨树慵懒地使淡白的树叶，
　　沙沙作响，发出银色的光芒，
或者像永不平静的大海翻滚的泡沫，
波浪在疾飞的海风中露出白牙闪亮。

她的金色头发洒落在金色的墙壁上，
　　好像精致的薄纱缠绕
在万寿菊锃亮的花盘上，
　　或者像向日葵转脸迎接太阳，
　　此时嫉妒的夜晚的阴郁已经结束，
百合花萌发的嫩枝散发晕光。

她的甜蜜的红嘴唇印在我的嘴唇上，
　　燃烧着红宝石一般的火焰，
摇曳不定的灯光在深红色的神龛，
　　或者像石榴花流血的创伤，
　　或者像绿荷红莲的花心水珠点点，
玫瑰红葡萄酒似血汁一样斟满。

George Gordon Byron (1788-1824)

She Walks in Beauty

She walks in beauty, like the night
Of cloudless climes and starry skies;
And all that's best of dark and bright
Meet in her aspect and her eye;
Thus mellowed to that tender light
Which heaven to gaudy day denies.

One shade the more, one ray the less
Had half impaired the nameless grace
Which waves in every raven tress,
Or softly lightens o'er her face;
Where thoughts serenely sweet express
How pure, how dear their dwelling-place.

And on that cheek, and o'er that brow,
So soft, so calm, yet eloquent,
The smiles that win, the tints that glow,
But tell of days in goodness spent,
A mind at peace with all below,
A heart whose love is innocent.

她在美中徜徉

［英］乔治·戈登·拜伦

她在美中徜徉，好像夜空
皎洁无云，繁星闪烁；
所有明与暗的最美色泽，
在她面容和眼波中辉映交错；
如此丰润融化成柔和的光，
上天难以承受这白天的艳丽。

多一分阴影，少一分光芒，
会损失不可名状的魅力，
在她乌黑的头发上波动，
她面庞娇柔而神采奕奕；
宁静亲切地表达思绪，
其心地多么纯粹，多么亲密。

在脸颊上，在额头上，
如此恬柔，如此娴静而动人，
迷人的微笑，明亮的肤色，
流露出度过的温馨岁月，
平和的心态宽宏大度，
充满爱情的心真诚无邪！

Wild Nights—Wild Nights

Emily Dickinson (1830-1886)

Wild Nights—Wilds Nights!
WereI with thee
Wild Nights should be
Our luxury!

Futile—the winds—
To a Heart in port—
Done with the Compass—
Done with the chart!

Rowing in Eden—
Ah, the Sea!
Might I moor—Tonight—
In Thee!

暴风雨之夜

［美］艾米莉·狄金森

暴风雨之夜——暴风雨之夜！
如果我与你同在一起
暴风雨之夜应该是
我们的极乐世界！

狂风——枉费气力——
心已经在港湾栖息——
指南针放下——
航海图收起！

泛舟伊甸园——
啊，海洋！
但愿我可停泊——今晚——
在你心上！

Bright Star

John Keats (1795-1821)

Bright star! would I were steadfast as thou art—
Not in lone splendour hung aloft the night
And watching, with eternal lids apart,
Like nature's patient, sleepless Eremite,
The moving waters at their priestlike task
Of pure ablution round earth's human shores,
Or gazing on the new soft-fallen mask
Of snow upon the mountains and the moors—
No—yet still steadfast, still unchangeable,
Pillow'd upon my fair love's ripening breast,
To feel forever its soft fall and swell,
Awake forever in a sweet unrest,
Still, still to hear her tender-taken breath,
And so live ever—or else swoon to death.

明亮的星

[英] 约翰·济慈

明亮的星啊！我愿如你一样坚定不移——
不愿独自辉煌悬挂在夜空天宇，
像大自然的有耐力的不眠隐士，
以永久的眼睑分离，睁眼注视
流动的海水担负牧师般的使命，
为地球人类彼岸进行圣洁的洗礼，
或者凝视初雪纷纷扬扬轻轻落下
覆盖在山脉和荒原上一望无际——
啊！不——我依然坚定，依然始终不渝，
头枕着我美丽爱人成熟的乳峰，
永远感觉它温柔的膨胀和起伏，
永远苏醒感到一种激荡的甜蜜，
静静地，依然倾听她那娇柔的呼吸，
就这样永远活着——或者在昏迷中死去。

Sara Teasdale (1884-1933)

The Rose and the Bee

If I were a bee and you were a rose,
Would you let me in when the gray wind blows?
Would you hold your petals wide apart,
Would you let me in to find your heart,
    If you were a rose?

"If I were a rose and you were a bee,
You should never go when you came to me,
I should hold my love on my heart at last,
I should close my leaves and keep you fast,
    If you were a bee."

玫瑰和蜜蜂

[美]莎拉·蒂斯黛尔

如果我是蜜蜂，你是玫瑰，
当寒风狂吹时你是否让我进来？
但愿你将你的花瓣大大张开，
但愿你让我进来发现你的心怀，
　　如果你是一朵玫瑰？

“如果我是玫瑰，你是蜜蜂，
但愿你来到我身边决不远行，
我应该在我心中始终保持我的爱，
我应该关闭我的叶片只等你来临，
　　如果你是一只蜜蜂。”

Dream Girl

Carl Sandburg (1878-1967)

You will come one day in a waver of love,
Tender as dew, impetuous as rain,
The tan of the sun will be on your skin,
The purr of the breeze in your murmuring speech,
You will pose with a hill-flower grace.

You will come, with your slim, expressive arms,
A poise of the head no sculptor has caught
And nuances spoken with shoulder and neck,
Your face in a pass-and-repass of moods
As many as skies in delicate change
Of cloud and blue and flimmering sun.

Yet ,

You may not come, O girl of a dream,
We may but pass as the world goes by
And take from a look of eyes into eyes,
A film of hope and a memoried day.

梦中情人

［美］卡尔·桑德堡

你将会来到，在爱情摇摆中的一天，
像露珠一样娇柔，像暴雨一样猛烈，
太阳将黝黑印上你的皮肤，
你喃喃低语中有一阵轻声柔意，
你将摆出山花般优雅姿势。

你将会来到，挥舞你富有表情的修长手臂，
雕塑家无法捕捉你头部的风韵，
也不能分辨你用肩膀和头颈说话的微妙差别，
你的面容在反复无常的情绪中
如同天空一样无穷地千变万化，
白云和蓝天和时隐时现的太阳。

但是，
你可能不来，哦，一个梦中情人，
我们可能只是像世人一样擦肩而过，
撷取从眼神到眼睛的一瞥，
一部希望的影片和一个值得回忆的日子。

I Think of Thee

Elizabeth Barrett Browning (1806-1861)

I think of thee —my thoughts do twine and bud
About thee, as wild vines, about a tree,
Put out broad leaves, and soon there's nought to see
Except the straggling green which hides the wood.
Yet, O my palm-tree, be it understood
I will not have my thoughts instead of thee
Who art dearer, better! Rather, instantly
Renew thy presence; as a strong tree should,
Rustle thy boughs and set thy trunk all bare,
And let these bands of greenery which insphere thee
Drop heavily down,—burst, shattered, everywhere!
Because, in this deep joy to see and hear thee
And breathe within thy shadow a new air,
I do not think of thee—I am too near thee.

我想念你

［英］伊丽莎白·巴雷特·勃朗宁

我想念你——我的思绪像小花和细枝
围绕你，如同野生藤蔓缠绕树木，
长出宽大叶子，很快会一叶障目，
只能看到隐藏在树林蔓延的绿色。
但是，哦，要明白，我的棕榈树，
我不愿我的思绪替代你，而失去
更珍贵，更亲的你！最好，立即
更新你的存在；像一棵挺拔的树，
你的树枝沙沙作响，露出你的树干，
挣脱包围你的这些绿荫的绳索，
让它沉重落下——轰然散开，撒落一地！
因为，充溢这深切的欢乐看见和听见你，
在你的阴影中呼吸清新的空气，
我再不想念你——我要紧紧贴近你。

I Hid My Love

John Clare (1793-1864)

I hid my love when young while I
Couldn't bear the buzzing of a fly;
I hid my love to my despite
Till I could not bear to look at light.
I dare not gaze upon her face
But left her memory in each place,
Where ere I saw a wildflower lie
I kissed and bade my love goodbye.

I met her in the greenest dells
Where dewdrops pearl the wood bluebells;
The lost breeze kissed her bright blue eye
The bee kissed and went singing by.
A sunbeam found a passage there,
A gold chain round her neck so fair;
As secret as the wild bee's song,
She lay there all the summer long.

I hid my love in field and town
Till e'en the breeze would knock me down;
The bees seemed singing ballads o'er
The fly's buss turned a lion's roar.
And even silence found a tongue
To haunt me all the summer long;
The riddle nature could not prove
Was nothing else but secret love.

John Clare (1793-1864)

我的暗恋

年轻时我曾经暗恋过，我不能
忍受一只渺小飞虫的嗡嗡噪音；
我暗恋着以免引起对我的轻视，
直到我不能忍受看见一线光明。
我真的不敢直眼凝视她的面庞，
可每一个地方都留下她的倩影；
无论何处我看到一朵野花绽放，
我都吻一下与我的爱道别一声。

我在翠绿色的小山谷遇见她，
树林子里风铃草缀满了露滴；
迷途的微风吻她明亮蓝眼睛，
蜜蜂亲吻她一路欢唱着飞去，
一缕阳光穿透了层层的密叶，
她围着金链的颈项如此白皙；
如同野蜂唱的歌声那样隐秘，
她在那里躺了整个漫长夏季。

我暗恋我的爱在田野和乡镇，
直到弱不禁风，体力也不胜，
蜜蜂似乎一遍遍地唱着歌谣，
飞虫低哼变成狮吼让人吃惊；
甚至寂静也能找到舌头发声，
使我整个漫长夏季不得安宁；
大自然都不能破解这个谜语，
这是暗恋，这就是秘密爱情。

［英］约翰·克莱尔

The Ragged Wood

O hurry where by water among trees
The delicate-stepping stag and his lady sigh,
When they have but looked upon their images—
O that none ever loved but you and I !

Or have you heard that sliding silver-shoed
Pale silver-proud queen-woman of the sky,
When the sun looked out of his golden hood—
O that none ever loved but you and I !

O hurry to the ragged wood, for there
I will drive all those lovers out and cry—
O my share of the world, O yellow hair!
No one has ever loved but you and I .

蓊郁的树林

［爱尔兰］威廉·巴特勒·叶芝

哦，快点到树林间的溪水边，
步态优雅的牡鹿和他的夫人叹息，
他们只看见自己的倒映在水面——
哦，除了你和我，不曾有人爱过！

或者，你听说天上穿银鞋滑行
银装闪亮的王后般的白皙妇女，
太阳从金色的风帽中朝外观望——
哦，除了你和我，不曾有人爱过！

哦，快点到蓊郁的树林，因为在那里，
我将驱赶所有的恋人们出来，并呼喊——
哦，我的一份世界，哦，金黄色的头发！
除了你和我，不曾有人爱过。

这首歌谣式的抒情诗，唱出所有情人的不可动摇的信念：开始都是以为“除了你和我，不曾有人爱过”。

Meeting at Night

The gray sea and the long black land;
And the yellow half-moon large and low;
And the startled little waves that leap
In fiery ringlets from their sleep,
As I gain the cove with pushing prow,
And quench its speed i' the slushy sand.

Then a mile of warm sea-scented beach;
Three fields to cross till a farm appears;
A tap at the pane, the quick sharp scratch
And blue spurt of a lighted match,
And a voice less loud, through its joys and fears,
Than the two hearts beating each to each!

幽会

［英］罗伯特·勃朗宁

灰蒙蒙的海洋，黑黢黢的陆地；
金黄的半月大而低垂挂在天边；
大海在闪亮的涟漪的睡眠中，
惊起的小浪跳跃着波光涟涟，
随即我调转船头驶进了小湾，
熄火减速擦着泥泞靠近沙滩。

走上一英里温暖的海味的海岸；
穿过三块田才看到农舍田庄；
轻叩窗户，接着急速尖声刮擦，
点着火柴发出蓝色火花光芒，
一个低嗓音，透着欢乐和害怕，
只听到彼此两颗心跳动怦怦响！

他们俩是传奇的维多利亚罗曼史：一个是已度过了她的青春的病弱女子，另一个则是精力充沛的英俊青年诗人，他带她出走意大利，在托斯卡纳阳光下，他们的爱情迅速发展，创作获得丰硕成果。勃朗宁夫人病体康复。他们的诗反映两个人截然不同的视角：她是赞美他们的爱情，而他更多的是唤起激动人心的约会。

William Carlos Williams (1883-1963)

Love Song

I lie here thinking of you—

the stain of love
is upon the world!
Yellow, yellow, yellow
it eats into the leaves,
smears with saffron
the horned branches that lean
heavily
against a smooth purple sky!
There is no light
only a honey-thick stain
that drips from leaf to leaf
and limb to limb
spoiling the colors
of the whole world—

you far off there under
the wine-red selvage of the west!

情歌

［美］威廉·卡洛斯·威廉斯

我躺在这里思念着你——

爱情的色斑
在这世界上！
黄色，黄色，黄色
它蚕食了这些叶子，
污迹带有橘黄色
倾斜的角状枝条
重重地
倚靠着光滑的紫色天空！
没有光
只有黏稠的蜂蜜污迹
滴落从叶片到叶片
从树枝到树枝
糟蹋整个世界的
色彩——

你遥远地在那里
在西方的酒红色的边缘！

Edna St. Vincent Millay (1893-1950)

[美] 埃德娜·圣·文森特·米莱

Ebb

I know what my heart is like
　Since your love died:
It is like a hollow ledge
　Holding a little pool
Left there by the tide,
　A little tepid pool,
Drying inward from edge.

退潮

我知道我的心像什么
　因为你的爱情消逝：
它像是暗礁上的凹洼
　托起一个小水坑
涨潮时积留在那儿，
　一个微温的小水坑，
正在从边缘向内里干涸。

Mucha

Mucha

Mucha

Mucha

LA·DAME·
AUX·CAMELIAS
SARAH BERNHARDT
Mucha
THEATRE DE LA
RENAISSANCE

LORENZACCIO
D'ALFRED DE MUSSET
ANNO DOMINI
SARAH BERNHARDT
MDCCCXCVI
Mucha
THEATRE DE LA
RENAISSANCE

Mucha

Mucha

Oh, When I was in Love

Alfred Edward Housman (1859-1936)
[英] 阿尔弗雷德·爱德华·豪斯曼

Oh, when I was in love with you,
  Then I was clean and brave,
And miles around the wonder grew
  How well did I behave.

And now the fancy passes by,
  And nothing will remain,
And miles around they'll say that I
  Am quite myself again.

啊，当我恋爱时

啊，当我爱上你的时候，
  我是多么勇敢和整洁，
周围的人们都惊叹不已，
  我的行为举止大方得体。

现在对你的迷恋已经过去，
  也没有留下什么痕迹，
周围的人们就异口同声说，
  我完全再一次做回自己。

Leigh Hunt (1784-1859)

Jenny Kiss'd Me

Jenny kiss'd me when we met,
  Jumping from the chair she sat in;
Time, you thief, who love to get
  Sweets into your list, put that in!
Say I'm weary, say I'm sad,
  Sat that health and wealth have miss'd me,
Say I'm growing old, but add,
  Jenny kiss'd me.

詹妮吻了我

[英]李·亨特

我们相见时詹妮吻了我，
　她从座椅上一跃而起；
时间，你这个窃贼，喜欢
　将快乐列入你的账本里！
说我疲乏无力，说我消沉，
　说健康和财富已经离我而去，
说我正在变老，但加上一句，
　詹妮吻了我。

李·亨特是19世纪英国诗人与批评家。这首诗的詹妮是历史学家和散文家托马斯·卡莱尔（Thomas Carlyle）的妻子。

Elizabeth Barrett Browning (1806-1861)

First Time He Kissed Me

First time he kissed me, he but only kissed
The fingers of this hand wherewith I write;
And ever since, it grew more clean and white,
Slow to world-greetings, quick with its "Oh, list,"
When the angels speak. A ring of amethyst
I could not wear here, plainer to my sight,
Than that first kiss. The second passed in height
The first, and sought the forehead, and half missed,
Half falling on the hair. O beyond meed!
That was the chrism of love, which love's own crown,
With sanctifying sweetness, did precede.
The third upon my lips was folded down
In perfect, purple state; since when, indeed,
I have been proud and said, "My love, my own."

第一次他吻我

[英]伊丽莎白·巴蕾特·勃朗宁

第一次他吻我，他只是把我
用以写作的这只手的手指亲一亲；
从此后，手指变得更加白皙和干净，
我不会世俗寒暄，只喜欢招呼“啊，快听，
听天使在说话”。这时我即使戴上
紫水晶戒指，在我看来，也不能
比第一个吻更珍贵。第二个吻超过
第一个高度，寻找前额，只有半个吻，
一半吻到发丝。啊，报偿已更亲近！
这是爱神的宝贵皇冠，爱神的圣油洗淋，
带着神圣的甜蜜，优于先前的吻。
第三个互相重叠，紧紧印在我的双唇
十分完美，美妙无比；从那时起，当真，
我骄傲地说：“我的爱人，我的自己人。”

I Love My Love in the Morning

Gerald Griffin (1803-1840)

I love my love in the morning,
For she like morn is fair—
Her blushing cheek, its crimson steak,
It clouds her golden hair.
Her glance, its beam, so soft and kind;
Her tears, its dewy showers;
And her voice, the tender whispering wind
That stirs the early bowers.

I love my love in the morning,
I love my love at noon,
For she is bright as the lord of light,
Yet mild as autumn's moon;
Her beauty is my bosom's sun,
Her faith my fostering shade,
And I will love my darling one,
Till even the sun shall fade.

I love my love in the morning,
　I love my love at even;
Her smile's soft play is like the ray
　That lights the western heaven:
I loved her when the sun was high,
　I loved her when he rose;
But best of all when evening's sigh
　Was murmuring at its close.

Gerald Griffin (1803-1840)

我爱我的爱人在早晨

我爱我的爱人在早晨，
　她像清晨这么瑰丽——
她的脸颊绯红多妩媚，
　金色头发如天云晨曦。
她的目光如此柔和友善；
　她的眼泪如露珠欲滴；
她的嗓音温柔如微风私语
　在这清早的闺房里洋溢。

我爱我的爱人在早晨，
　我爱我的爱人在正午，
因为她明亮如光明之王，
　又如秋天皎月缀在天幕；
她的美丽是我内心的太阳，
　她的信仰将我心灵培育，
我将爱我的心上人，
　甚至直到太阳下坠沉没。

我爱我的爱人在早晨，
　我爱我的爱人在夜晚；
她的微笑温柔动人
　好像霞光辉耀西天：
我爱她，当太阳当空高挂，
　我爱她，当太阳冉冉上升；
但一切最好的是夜晚的叹息，
　是窃窃私语亲密时分。

Love and Sleep

Algernon Charles Swinburne (1837-1909)

Lying asleep between the strokes of night
  I saw my love lean over my sad bed,
  Pale as the duskiest lily's leaf or head,
Smooth-skinned and dark, with bare throat made to bite,
Too wan for blushing and too warm for white,
  But perfect-coloured without white or red.
  And her lips opened amorously, and said—
I wist not what, saving one word—Delight.

And all her face was honey to my mouth,
  And all her body pasture to mine eyes;
    The long lithe arms and hotter hands than fire,
The quivering flanks, hair smelling of the south,
  The bright light feet, the splendid supple thighs
    And glittering eyelids of my soul's desire.

爱情与睡眠

[英]阿尔杰农·查尔斯·史文朋

在夜晚的轻抚下躺下安睡
　我看见我爱人倚靠在我悲伤的床头，
　苍白如最忧郁的百合花叶片或叶球，
微暗的光滑皮肤，裸露的脖颈紧紧依偎，
赧颜太无血色，白皙又太温热，
　只是没有白或红的完美色彩。
　她的嘴唇含情脉脉张开，诉说——
我听不清，说出一个单词——快乐。

她的整个脸颊贴到我嘴里是蜂蜜，
　她的整个身体在我的眼里是草地；
　　比火更热的手，长长的圆润双臂，
柔韧的腰肢，头发散发南方的气息，
　玲珑轻盈纤足，丰腴柔软双腿
　　闪闪发亮的眼睛透出灵魂的渴望。

The Silken Tent

Robert Frost (1874-1963)

She is as in a field a silken tent
At midday, when a sunny summer breeze
Has dried the dew, and all its ropes relent
So that in guys it gently sways at ease
And its supporting central cedar pole
That is its pinnacle to heavenward
And signifies the sureness of the soul
Seems to owe naught to any single cord
But, strictly held by none, is loosely bound
By countless silken ties of love and thought
To everything on earth the compass round
And only by one going slightly taut
In the capriciousness of summer air
Is of the slightest bondage made aware.

丝质帐篷

她如同田野上的一顶丝质帐篷，
阳光灿烂正午时分，一阵夏日微风
吹干露珠，它的所有绳索变得松软，
就这样它在拉索中可随意轻轻摇动，
而它那中央雪杉木的支撑柱杆
是那朝向高高天空的帐篷顶端，
那是标志灵魂的确信，稳定安全，
似乎与任何一根绳子都没有牵连，
完全不受任何牵掣，松松地
由无数爱慕和思念的丝带绑定，
与地球万物绕行，浑然一体，
只有当某一根丝带轻轻拉紧，
在夏日天空的风云变幻里，
最轻微的束缚才会使它有所意识。

罗伯特·弗罗斯特是20世纪美国最受尊崇的诗人之一。全诗似一个长句。弗罗斯特将一种古老的诗歌形式——十四行诗与独特的现代口语化语言结合，形成他作品的典型特点。作为隐喻大师，他创造了一种超级感官的效果，描写女人动人之处，如夏日微风中的一顶丝质帐篷一样。这首诗感情丰富而朦胧。诗人晚年将诗送给他的秘书Kay，后者曾抄录此诗。

Dorothy Parker (1893-1967)

One Perfect Rose

A single flow'r he sent me, since we met,
All tenderly his messenger he chose;
Deep-hearted, pure, with scented dew still wet-
One perfect rose.

I knew the language of the floweret;
'My fragile leaves,'it said,'his heart enclose.'
Love long has taken for his amulet
One perfect rose.

Why is it no one ever sent me yet
One perfect limousine, do you suppose?
Ah no, it's always just my luck to get
One perfect rose.

一朵完美的玫瑰

［美］多萝茜·帕克

自从我们相遇他送我花一朵。
　他温柔体贴选择自己的信使；
内心深处纯洁，清新露珠圆润
　一朵完美的玫瑰。

因为我懂得这些花语；
　它说：“我脆弱的叶子，他用心呵护。”
爱长久地用作他的护身符
　一朵完美的玫瑰。

你猜度一下，为什么从来没有人
　送给我一台完美的豪车？
啊不，这一定是我的运气，赢得
　一朵完美的玫瑰。

Sara Teasdale (1884-1933)

Less Than the Cloud to the Wind

Less than the cloud to the wind,
    Less than the foam to the sea,
Less than the rose to the storm
    Am I to thee.

More than the star to the night,
    More than the rain to the lea,
More than heaven to earth
    Art thou to me.

云朵小于狂风

［美］莎拉·蒂斯黛尔

云朵小于狂风，
泡沫小于大海，
玫瑰小于风暴
我小于你。

星星大于夜晚，
暴雨大于草地，
天空大于大地
你大于我。

Gifts

Juliana Horatia Ewing (1841-1885)

You ask me what since we must part
You shall bring back to me.
Bring back a pure and faithful heart
As true as mine to thee.

You talk of gems from foreign lands,
Of treasure, spoil, and prize.
Ah love! I shall not search your hands
But look into your eyes.

礼物

[英] 朱丽安娜·赫拉提亚·尤因

每次离别你问我要什么礼物
你都会带回来向我奉献。
我只要你带回一颗纯洁忠诚的心
像我给你的一样纯真缠绵。

你谈到外国的珍珠宝贝，
这些尽是财富、珠宝和珍品。
啊，亲爱的！我不会搜索你的双手，
我只会注视你的这双眼睛。

1867年6月，朱丽安娜嫁给陆军上尉亚历山大·尤因。他们开始生活，一起旅行。后来朱丽安娜病倒，大约1879年回到伦敦。她的丈夫继续在世界各地辗转。这首诗描写的是在这些分离的年头里朱丽安娜的思想。

A Birthday

My heart is like a singing bird
   Whose nest is in a watered shoot;
My heart is like an apple tree
   Whose boughs are bent with thickset fruit;
My heart is like a rainbow shell
   That paddles in a halcyon sea;
My heart is gladder than all these
   Because my love is come to me.

Raise me a dais of silk and dawn;
   Hang it with vair and purple dyes;
Carve it in doves, and pomegranates,
   And peacocks with a hundred eyes;
Work it in gold and silver grapes,
   In leaves, and silver fleur-de-lys;
Because the birthday of my life
   Is come, my love is come to me.

生日

［英］克里斯蒂娜·罗塞蒂

我的心好像是只唱歌的鸟
　窝巢筑在湿润的嫩枝上；
我的心好像是棵苹果树，
　密实的果实压弯摇晃的树枝；
我的心好像彩虹贝壳，
　在宁静的大海上荡漾；
我的心比这一切都快乐，
　因为我的爱人来到我身旁。

为我安放一台丝绒高座，
　挂上金色和紫色罗帐；
在上面雕刻鸽子和石榴，
　还有孔雀眼睛一百双；
镶上金色和银色的葡萄，
　用树叶和银色鸢尾草包装；
因为我一生的生日来临，
　我的爱人来到我的身旁。

Betwixt Mine Eye and Heart a League Is Took

William Shakespeare (1564-1616)

Betwixt mine eye and heart a league is took,
And each doth good turns now unto the other:
When that mine eye is famish'd for a look,
Or heart in love with sighs himself doth smother,
With my love's picture then my eye doth feast
And to the painted banquet bids my heart.
Another time mine eye is my heart's guest.
And in his thoughts of love doth share a part.
So either by thy picture or my love,
Thyself away art present still with me;
For thou no farther than my thoughts canst move,
And I am still with them, and they with thee;
    Or if they sleep, thy picture in my sight
    Awakes my heart, to heart's and eye's delight.

我的眼与心之间结为同盟

[英] 威廉·莎士比亚

现在我的眼与心之间结为同盟，
约定彼此要给予对方爱的便利：
当我的眼睛渴望一睹你的面容，
或者我的爱心不胜唏嘘而郁悒，
当我的眼睛享受我爱人的肖像，
就邀请我的心光临这图画大餐；
下次我的心约请眼睛做客府上
将会共同分享它对爱人的思念：
这样，既靠我的恋情又靠你的图像，
你本人虽远离他方依然和我在一起；
你走得再远我的思念也会紧随跟上，
思念与你同在，我永远与思念在一起；
　　如果思念睡着了，在我眼前，你的肖像
　　唤醒我的心，使心和眼一起欣喜若狂。

诗人利用艺术创造的形象（图像、绘画）和心中保存的形象（意念、本性）之间的差别与统一，思念爱人。此诗印证谚语：“与人分享，快乐加倍，悲伤减半。”

Charles Best (1570-1627)

A Sonnet of the Moon

Look how the pale queen of the silent night
Doth cause the ocean to attend upon her,
And he, as long as she is in his sight,
With her full tide is ready her to honor.
But when the silver waggon of the moon
Is mounted up so high he cannot follow,
The sea calls home his crystal waves to moan,
And with low ebb doth manifest his sorrow.
So you that are the sovereign of my heart
Have all my joys attending on your will;
My joys low-ebbing when you do depart,
When you return their tide my heart doth fill.
So as you come and as you do depart,
Joys ebb and flow within my tender heart.

月亮十四行

[英] 查尔斯·贝斯特

瞧，寂静夜晚的苍白女王
大海诚惶诚恐服侍在她身旁，
而大海，只要她在眼前出现，
以满潮迎接她驾临的荣光。
但当月亮银色的四轮马车
直入云霄，大海不能追随跟上，
他呼唤月亮回家，用水晶波浪的呜咽，
并用低潮显示无限悲怆。
我的所有快乐按照你的旨意出现
月亮啊，你是我心中的君王；
你离开时我的快乐也陷入低潮，
你回来时我心中也会欢乐无量。
你这样来到又这样去向远方，
快乐潮水在我温柔的心中激荡。

Farewell, Ungrateful Traitor!

John Dryden (1631-1700)

Farewell, ungrateful traitor!
   Farewell, my perjured swain!
Let never injured woman
   Believe a man again.
The pleasure of possessing
Surpasses all expressing,
But 'tis too short a blessing,
   And love too long a pain.

'Tis easy to deceive us
   In pity of your pain,
But when we love, you leave us
   To rail at you in vain.
Before we have descried it,
There is no joy beside it,
But she that once has tried it
   Will never love again.

The passion you pretended
　Was only to obtain,
But when the charm is ended
　The charmer you disdain.
Your love by ours we measure
Till we have lost our treasure,
But dying is a pleasure,
　When living is a pain.

别了，忘恩负义的负心汉！

别了，忘恩负义的负心汉！
　别了，我虚情假意的情郎！
决不让受到伤害的姑娘
　再一次轻信一个男人。
这种占有带来的快乐
无法用语言形容表达，
但是这种幸福总是太短促
　爱却是一种太长久的痛苦。

欺骗我们实在太容易
　只要对你的痛苦深表同情，
但我们一爱上，你抛弃我们
　抱怨你也是徒劳枉然。
在我们辨别真假以前，
那就没有什么快乐可言，
但是她一旦尝试过苦果
　将永远不会再真心相爱。

你伪装得满腔激情

　只是为了骗人得手，

但当姑娘魅力一旦消失

　你就会弃如敝履。

我们用我们的爱权衡你的爱

我们往往会丧失无价之宝，

假如活着总是痛苦，

　死亡就会成为解脱。

The Mess of Love

We've made a great mess of love
Since we made an ideal of it.

The moment I swear to be a woman, a certain woman,all my life
That moment I begin to hate her.

The moment I even say to a woman: I love you!—
My love dies down considerably.

The moment love is an understood thing between us, we are sure of it,
It's cold egg, it isn't love any more.

Love is like a flower, it must flower and fade;
If it doesn't fade, it is not a flower,
It's either an artificial rag blossom, or an immortelle, for

the cemetery.

The moment the mind interferes with love, or the will fixes
on it,
Or the personality assumes it as an attribute, or the ego
takes possession of it,
It is not love any more, it's just a mess.
And we've made a great mess of love, mind-perverted,
will-perverted, ego-perverted love.

爱情困境

我们创造了一个爱情大困境
因为我们臆造了一个爱情理想。

我发誓我一辈子爱上一个女人、某个女人的时刻，
这也是我开始怨恨她的时刻。

甚至这个时刻，我对一个女人说：我爱你！——
我的爱情就相当程度地渐渐开始流失。

爱情是我们之间心照不宣、我们确信的时刻，
它就变成一个冰冷的鸡蛋，它不再是爱。

爱情像是一朵花，它必须是鲜花并会凋谢；
假如它不会凋谢，它就不是花，
它就是墓地用的人造布花，或是蜡花。

心灵干扰爱情或者意志修复爱情的时刻，

或者个人假设它是一个属性，或者自我占有它的时刻，

它不再是爱情，它只是一个困境。

我们创造了一个爱情大困境，心灵误解的、意志误解的、

自我误解的爱情大困境。

劳伦斯与他的妻子弗里达（Frieda）有一段骚乱不安的婚姻。他们不断地争斗。主要是因为他们的风流韵事，将引起弗里达失去与前夫所生育的孩子的监护权。

Heart, We Will Forget Him

Emily Dickinson (1830-1886)

Heart, we will forget him!
   You and I , tonight!
You may forget the warmth he gave,
   I will forget the light.

When you have done, pray tell me,
   That I my thoughts may dim;
Haste! lest while you're lagging,
   I may remember him!

心啊，我们要忘记他

［美］艾米莉·迪金森

心啊，我们要忘记他！
　你和我，就在今天晚上！
你要忘记他给的温暖，
　我也要忘记这束光亮。

你忘记时，请告诉我，
　我的想法有点犹疑；
赶快！免得你落在后面，
　我可能会又把他记起！

艾米莉受过良好教育，终身未嫁。她一生写了1800多首诗，藏之于箱底，生前只发表了8首，后来亲友把她的赠诗私自拿出去匿名发表。据说，诗中也有描述失败恋情的。她死后声名远播，文学成就无以复加。

The Rival

Sylvia Plath (1932-1963)

If the moon smiled, she would resemble you,
You leave the same impression
Of something beautiful, but annihilating.
Both of you are great light borrowers.
Her O-mouth grieves at the world; your is unaffected,

And your first gift is making stone out of everything.
I wake to a mausoleum; you are here,
Ticking your fingers on the marble table, looking for cigarettes,
Spiteful as a woman, but nor so nervous,
And dying to say something unanswerable.

The moon, too, abases her subjects,
But in the daytime she is ridiculous.
Your dissatisfactions, on the other hand,
Arrive through the mailslot with loving regularity,
White and blank, expansive as carbon monoxide.

No day is safe from news of you,
Walking about in Africa maybe, but thinking of me.

对手

[美] 希维亚·普拉斯

如果月亮微笑，她会像你一样。
你留下同样的印象，
美丽却具有毁灭性。
你俩都是出色的光的借用者。
她的O形嘴为这个世界悲伤；你的却无动于衷。

你旷世奇才是把一切变成石头。
我醒来面对一座陵墓；你在这儿，
手指在大理石桌上叩打，想找香烟，
怀恨在心如同一个女人，但没那么神经质，
死命想说出无法回答的话语。

月亮也贬抑她的臣民，
但在白天她荒唐可笑。
另一方面，你的不悦，
怀有爱意通过大批邮件定期送达，
白色和空洞，扩散如一氧化碳。

没有一天能够逃避你的消息，
你也许在非洲漫游，却想着我。

Untitled

If grief for grief can touch thee,
If answering woe for woe,
If any ruth can melt thee,
Come to me now!

I cannot be more lonely,
More drear I cannot be!
My worn heart throbs so wildly
'Twill break for thee.

And when the world despises,
When heaven repels my prayer,
Will not mine angel comfort?
Mine idol hear?

Yes, by the tears I've poured thee,
By all my hours of pain,
I shall surely win thee,
Beloved, again!

无题

[英] 艾米莉·勃朗特

如果以悲伤为悲伤可以触动你，
如果以痛苦为痛苦可以回应你，
如果任何同情可以融化你，
请马上来到我这里！

我再也不能孤苦伶仃，
我再也不能郁郁不乐！
我疲累的心狂暴悸动
它将为你焦虑而心碎。

如果世人如此藐视轻蔑，
如果老天嫌弃我的祈祷，
我的天使不会安慰我吗？
我的偶像不会倾听我吗？

是的，我用眼泪向你倾诉，
在我所有的痛苦时刻，
我必将赢得你的回首，
心爱的人呵，再一次！

The Day Is Gone, and All Its Sweets Are Gone!

John Keats (1795-1821)

The day is gone, and all its sweets are gone!
  Sweet voice, sweet lips, soft hand, and softer breast,
Warm breath, light whisper, tender semi-tone,
  Bright eyes, accomplish'd shape, and lang'rous waist!
Faded the flower and all its budded charms,
  Faded the sight of beauty from my eyes,
Faded the shape of beauty from my arms,
  Faded the voice, warmth, whiteness, paradise-
Vanish'd unseasonably at shut of eve,
  When the dusk holiday or holinight
Of fragrant-curtain'd love begins to weave
  The woof of darkness thick, for hid delight;
But, as I've read love's missal through to-day,
  He'll let me sleep, seeing I fast and pray.

那一天过去了，所有欢乐已经消逝！

[英] 约翰·济慈

那一天过去了，所有欢乐已经消逝！
　悦耳的嗓音、甜蜜的芳唇、温软的纤手、柔软的乳房，
温馨的呼吸、轻声的低语、柔和的半音，
　明亮的眼睛、完美的身材和绵软的腰肢！
消逝了花朵以及它的蓓蕾所蕴含的魅力，
　消逝了我眼中所有美丽的倩影，
消逝了我臂弯中美丽的形体，
　消逝了这个嗓音，热情，纯洁，
天堂在傍晚结束时不合时宜地消失，
　芳香的帷幔遮蔽的爱恋欢情，
在薄暮朦胧的假日或日夜开始编织
　暗黑的厚重织品，以便隐藏欣喜；
但是，因为我今天整日阅读爱的弥撒书，
　看着我斋戒而祈祷，他会让我安然睡去。

Charlotte Mew (1869-1928)

Rooms

I remember rooms that have had their part
In the steady slowing down of the heart.
The room in Paris, the room at Geneva,
The little damp room with the seaweed smell,
And that ceaseless maddening sound of the tide—
Rooms where for good or for ill—things died.
But there is the room where we(two) lie dead,
Though every morning we seem to wake and
might just as well seem to sleep again
As we shall somewhere in the other quieter, dustier bed
Out there in the sun—in the rain.

房间

[美]夏洛特·缪

如今心跳镇定地变慢，
　　我还记得那些有关联的客房。
那巴黎的房间，日内瓦的房间，
带有海藻味的潮湿小房间，
还有令人发狂的连续不断的潮汐声音——
　　无论那个房间，好还是不好——故事已经结束。
但在有个房间我们（俩）躺下并死去，
尽管每个早晨我们好像醒过来，
　就像我们好像重新入睡那样
　　正如我们在某个地方在其他更安静的满是灰尘的床上，
　　在那里，在阳光里——在雨水里。

Love's Secret

William Blake (1757-1827)

Never seek to tell thy love,
  Love that never told can be;
For the gentle wind does move
  Silently, invisibly.

I told my love, I told my love,
  I told her all my heart,
Trembling, cold, in ghastly fears,
  Ah, she did depart!

Soon after she was gone from me,
  A traveler came by,
Silently, invisibly:
  He took her with sigh.

爱情秘诀

［英］威廉·布莱克

永远不要表白你的爱情，
　　爱情决不可开诚布公；
就像微风缓缓吹过，
　　悄无声息，无影无踪。

我表白我的爱情，尽情表白，
　　我告诉她掏尽我的心怀，
我颤抖，灰心，担惊受怕，
　　啊！她却毅然走开！

她刚刚离开我不久，
　　一个过路人过来示意，
悄无声息，无影无踪，
　　他带走她，伴随一声叹息。

布莱克是神秘主义诗人，比起精英话语更信仰真挚感情。也许这儿的讯息是，话语与行动相比，弊大于利。真正的爱情是以其他形式表达的。

Christina Rossetti (1830-1894)

Song

When I am dead, my dearest,
　Sing no sad songs for me;
Plant thou no roses at my head,
　Nor shady cypress tree:
Be the green grass above me
　With showers and dewdrops wet;
And if thou wilt, remember,
　And if thou wilt, forget.

I shall not see the shadows,
　I shall not feel the rain;
I shall not hear the nightingale
　Sing on, as if in pain;
And dreaming through the twilight
　That doth not rise nor set,
Haply I may remember,
　And haply may forget.

歌

［英］克里希蒂娜·罗塞蒂

当我去世时，最亲爱的人，
　不要为我唱悲伤的歌，
你不要在我的墓地上种玫瑰，
　也不要种绿叶成荫的柏树：
在我的墓地种满如茵的绿草
　常有温润的微雨和露珠；
如果你愿意，请记住我，
　如果你愿意，请忘记我。

我将不会看见树的阴影，
　我也将不会感觉飘飞的雨滴；
我不会听到夜莺的歌唱，
　唱的歌，仿佛悲怆哭啼：
穿越晨昏朦胧的梦想
　不会出现也不会消失，
我也许可能会记得，
　我也许可能会忘记。

William Butler Yeats (1865-1939)

When You Are Old

When you are old and gray and full of sleep,
And nodding by the fire, take down this book,
And slowly read, and dream of the soft look
Your eyes had once, and of their shadows deep;

How many loved your moments of glad grace,
And loved your beauty with love false or true;
But one man loved the pilgrim soul in you,
And loved the sorrows of your changing face;

And bending down beside the glowing bars,
Murmur, a little sadly, how Love fled
And paced upon the mountains overhead
And hid his face amid a crowd of stars.

当你老了

［爱尔兰］威廉·巴特勒·叶芝

当你老了，头发灰白，睡意昏沉，
在炉火边打着盹，取下这本书，
慢慢地细读，追梦你的双目
曾有的柔和光彩，深邃晕影；

多少人爱你快乐优雅的时分，
爱你的美丽，无论假意或真情；
但有一人爱着你那朝圣者的心灵，
爱你那日益衰老的脸庞的伤痕；

俯身弯腰在火光熊熊的炉栅旁，
有点感伤地轻声诉说爱情的消逝
独自在头顶群山上从容蹀躞
在密密繁星中间隐藏他的脸庞。

1889 年，23 岁的叶芝结识了 22 岁的演员茅德·冈（Maud Gonne）。诗人对其一见钟情，一往情深。冈回绝叶芝求婚后，诗人于 1893 年发表这篇荡气回肠的诗作。描写的场景虽是虚构的，但是鲜活生动，饱含真挚浓烈的情感，至今人们仍从不同角度演绎这首诗。

'Tis the Last Rose of Summer

Thomas Moore (1779-1852)

'Tis the last rose of Summer,
Left blooming alone;
All her lovely companions
Are faded and gone;
No flower of her kindred,
No rosebud is nigh,
To reflect back her blushes,
Or give sigh for sigh!
I'll not leave thee, thou lone one,
To pine on the stem;
Since the lovely are sleeping,
Go sleep thou with them.
Thus kindly I scatter
Thy leaves o'er the bed
Where thy
Mates of the garden
Lie scentless and dead.

So soon may I follow,
When friendships decay,
And from Love's shining circle
The gems drop away!
When true hearts lie withered,
And fond ones are flown,
Oh! who would inhabit
This bleak world alone?

夏日里最后的玫瑰

Thomas Moore (1779-1852)

夏日里最后的玫瑰，
孤零零开花无人陪；
她的所有亲密伙伴
都已凋谢或者枯萎；
身旁没有同宗亲属，
也没有其他玫瑰花蕾，
不能映衬她绯红脸庞，
不能一同叹息相依偎！
我不能离你撒手而去，
让你独自在枝头憔悴；
美丽同伴已经长眠，
你将与他们一起安息。
我这样轻轻地撒落
你的花叶覆盖床帏
你的花园里的同伴
正悄无声息躺下沉睡。
而我马上也会跟随，

当真诚的友谊衰微，
爱情闪光的项链圈
最珍贵的宝石跌坠！
真诚的心已经远去，
最心爱的人远走高飞，
啊！谁会独自在这世上
经受住寒冷的悲催？

Christina Rossetti (1830-1894)

Remember

Remember me when I am gone away,
Gone far away into the silent land;
When you can no more hold me by the hand,
Nor I half turn to go, yet turning stay.
Remember me when no more day by day
You tell me of our future that you plann'd:
Only remember me; you understand
It will be late to counsel then or pray.
Yet if you should forget me for a while
And afterwards remember, do not grieve:
For if the darkness and corruption leave
A vestige of the thoughts that once I had,
Better by far you should forget and smile
Than that you should remember and be sad.

记住

[英]克里斯蒂娜·罗塞蒂

请记住我，当我离去时，
　去到远方静谧的土地；
　当你再不能牵住我的手，
我也不会转身欲去还留。
记住我，你再也不能每天告诉我
　你计划的我们未来：
　只是记住我；你应该理解
那时商量或祈求已经太晚。
然而如果你将忘记一时，
　以后又想起，请不要伤逝：
　因为如果已经黑暗和腐朽，
还留下我曾有的一丝思念痕迹，
我宁愿你忘怀而微笑，
　　也不愿你记住而悲戚。

In Memory of My Mother

Patrick Kavanagh (1905-1967)

You will have the road gate open, the front door ajar
The kettle boiling and a table set
By the window looking out at the sycamores—
And your loving heart lying in wait

For me coming up among the poplar trees.
You'll know my breathing and my walk
And it will be a summer evening on those roads
Lonely with leaves of thought.

We will be choked with the grief of things growing,
The silence of dark-green air
Life too rich—the nettles, docks and thistles
All answering the prodigal's prayer.

You will know I am coming though I send no word
For you were lover who could tell
A man's thoughts—my thoughts—though I hid them—
Through you I knew Woman and did not fear her spell.

回忆我的母亲

[爱尔兰] 帕特里克·卡瓦纳

你会把路边院门打开，前门半掩
把壶中的水烧开又把餐桌摆好
倚窗注视着那棵梧桐树——
你怀着爱心一直在等候我的回归

等待我出现在那片杨树林中。
你熟悉我的呼吸和我的步履
它将是在这些道路上的一个夏夜
孤独地与思想的叶片在一起。

我们将因悲伤的事日增而哽咽，
暗绿色的天空的寂寥
生活太丰富——荨麻、阔叶野草和蒺藜
一切都在回答浪子的祈祷。

你会知道我的到来尽管我没有发回一个字
因为你曾是爱人，可能预判
男人的思想——我的思想——尽管我闭口不言——
通过你，我也了解女人，不害怕她的怨言。

In Every Dream

In every dream thy lovely fratures rise;
    I see them in the sunshine of the day;
Thy form is flitting still before my eyes
    Where'er at eve I tread my lonely way;
    In every moaning wind I hear thee say
Sweet words of consolation, while thy sighs
Seem borne along on every blast that flies;
    I live,I talk with thee where'er I stray:

And yet thou never more shalt come to me
    On earth, for thou art in a world of bliss,
And fairer still—if fairer thou canst be—
    Than when thou bloomed'st for a while in this.
Few be my days of loneliness and pain
Until I meet in love with thee again.

每一场梦境

[英]威廉·巴恩斯

每一场梦境，你妩媚的容貌都会浮现；
　　我看见可亲的容颜在白天的阳光里；
你的风姿依然在我的眼前晃动
　　夜晚无论我在哪里独行踽踽；
　　在每阵凄厉的寒风中我听见你说
安慰的甜言蜜语，虽然你的叹息
似乎是一起承受每阵刮起的疾风；
　　我活着，我与你谈话，无论我漂泊何地：

然而在世上，你不会有更多次来到我身旁
　　因为你已经在极乐世界里，
而且你依然更美丽——但愿你能更美丽——
　　胜过你一生中青春焕发的时期。
我孤独和痛苦的日子终将消逝
直到我再次遇见，重新爱恋你。

Echo

Christina Rossetti (1830-1894)

Come to me in the silence of the night;
Come in the speaking silence of a dream;
Come with soft rounded cheeks and eyes as bright
As sunlight on a stream;
Come back in tears;
O memory, hope, love of finished years.

O dream how sweet, too sweet, too bitter sweet
Whose wakening should have been in Paradise,
Where souls brimful of love abide and meet;
Where thirsting longing eyes
Watch the slow door
That, opening, letting in, lets out no more.

Yet come to me in dreams; that I may live
My very life again though cold in death:
Come back to me in dreams, that I may give
Pulse for pulse, breath for breath:
Speak low, lean low,
As long ago, my love, how long ago?

回声

［英］克里斯蒂娜·罗塞蒂

在夜晚寂静中来到我身旁；
在梦境低语的寂静中进来；
温柔的圆润脸颊，双眼如此明亮，
仿佛溪流上的阳光霞彩；
泪水涟涟中归来，
哦，逝去岁月的记忆、希望和爱。

哦，美梦多么甜蜜，太甜蜜，太苦涩的甜蜜，
苏醒应该是在天国乐园，
灵魂满溢着爱的容忍和交集；
眼睛怀着渴望和期盼
注视那扇缓慢的门
开启着，进入，再没有出现。

梦境中依然来到我身旁，我可以重新
过着我的生活，尽管有死亡的寒意：
在梦境中回到我身旁，我可以给予
脉搏以脉搏，呼吸以呼吸：
低声说话，低身俯就，
像很久以前，我的爱人，多么久的前世？

Thomas Hardy (1840-1928)

The Voice

Woman much missed, how you call to me, call to me,
Saying that now you are not as you were
When you had changed from the one who was all to me,
But as at first, when our day was fair.

Can it be you that I hear? Let me view you, then,
Standing as when I drew near to the town
Where you would wait for me: yes, as I knew you then,
Even to the original air-blue gown!

Or is it only the breeze, in its listlessness
Travelling across the wet mead to me here,
You being ever dissolved to wan wistlessness.
Heard no more again far or near?

    Thus I; faltering forward,
    Leaves around me falling,
Wind oozing thin through the thorn from norward,
    And the woman calling.

呼唤声

[英]托马斯·哈代

深深怀念的女人哟，你呼唤我，呼唤我，
诉说你现在已经不是往昔的你，
对于我，你原是我的心爱，你已经改变，
但是最初，我们的日子晴朗甜美。

我听见的可是你？让我看看你，
你站着，像以往我进城时一样，
在那地方你会等我：是的，像当时我认识的你，
甚至记得原先的那件蔚蓝色衣裳！

或者，只是一阵暮气沉沉的微风，
穿越这湿润的草地吹到我跟前，
莫非你被永远放逐于虚无缥缈中，
无论远近，呼唤声再也不会被听见？

　　我就这样：蹒跚前行，
　　在我周围树叶纷纷飘零，
北风掠过荆棘林丛低弱回旋，
　　那女人呼唤声声。

本诗表达诗人对亡妻爱玛的眷念之情。

Edna St. Vincent Millay (1892-1950)
［美］埃德娜·圣·文森特·米莱

Sorrow

Sorrow like a ceaseless rain
Beats upon my heart.
People twist and scream in pain—
Dawn will find them still again;
This has neither wax nor wane,
Neither stop nor start.

悲伤

悲伤像连绵不断的雨
敲打我的心。
人们因痛苦扭曲而尖叫——
黎明依然再一次发现它们；
痛苦没有增大也没有缩小，
既没有停止又没有开始。

Love And Age

Walter Savage Landor (1775-1864)
[英] 瓦特·萨维奇·兰德

Loves flies with bow unstrung when Time appears,
And trembles at the approach of heavy years.
A few bright feathers leaves he in his flight,
Quite beyond recall, but not forgotten quite.

爱情与老年

当机会出现时，因弓箭无弦爱情消逝，
而担忧疲累的岁月接踵而来。
一生飞翔中，留下几根鲜艳的羽毛，
不能完全记起，但也不会完全忘记。

索引

Index of Poets

参考文献

· Appleseed Press Book Publishers. *Shakespeare's Sonnets: The Complete Illustrated Poems*. Kennebunkport:Gider Mill Press Book Publishers LLC.,2016.

· Kathleen Blease. *Love in Verse: Classic Poems of The Heart*. New York:The Random House Publishing Group,1998.

· Stephen Booth.*Shakespeare's Sonnets*. New Haven and London: Yale University Press, 1977.

· Sally Ann Brek and James Gordon Wakeman. *1001 Love Poems*. New York : Black Dog & Leventhal Publishers, 1996.

· *Sonnets From The Portuguese*.The Golden Eagle Press.

· Kate Farrell. *Art & Love, An Illustrated Anthology of Love Poetry*. Boston, New York and London: A Bultinch Press Book/Little, Brown and Co.1990.

· Jennifer Fox. *100 Classic Love Poems*. Kansas City, Sydney and London: Andrews McMeel Publishing, LLC, 2012.

· Robert Giroux.*The Book Known as Q: A consideration of Shakespeare's Sonnets*.New York:Vintage Books,1983.

· Margreta de Grazia. *Shakespeare's Sonnets*.New York. Barnes & Noble, Inc., 2011.

· John Gabriel Hunt. *365 Love Poems*. New York :

Gramercy Books,1993.
· Michael Irwin.*The Collected Poems of Thomas Hardy*. London: Wordsworth Poetry Library, 2006.
· Stephen Matterson.*The Complete Poems of Walt Whitman*.London:Wordsworth Poetry Library, 2006.
· Max Morris. *Classic Love Poems*. West Sussex: Summersdale Publishers Ltd, 2014.
· Max Morris. *Love Poems*. West Sussex: Summersdale Publishers Ltd, 2016.
· Leslie Pockell. *The 100 Best Love Poems of All Time*. New York: Warner Books, 2003.
· Gerald Dewitt Sanders,John Herbert Nelson and M. L. Rosenthal. *Chief Modern Poets of Britain and America*. New York and London: Macmillan Publishing Co., Inc., 1970.
· Jon Stallworthy. *A Book of Love Poetry*. New York: Oxford University Press, 1986.
· Charles Sullivan. *Loving: Poetry and Art*.New York: Harry N. Abrams, Inc., 1992.
· The Academy of American Poets. *365 Poems for Every Occasion*. New York: Abrams Image, 2015.
· Louis Untermeyer. *The Pocket Book of Robert Frost's Poems*. New York: Washington Square Press, Inc. 1969.
· Peter Washington. *Love Poems*. New York, London and Toronto: Everyman's Library, 1993.
· Jonathan Williams and Clive Cheesman. *The British Museum Classical Love Poetry*.London:The British Museum Press, 2013.

后记

POSTSCRIPT

凡事都要有缘分，无论是祸福吉凶或是悲欢离合，都离不开缘分。碰到类似这种“可遇不可求”的境遇，人只能顺应机缘，任其自然，所以，佛又有“随缘”的说法。缘分随处可见。例如，世人说，杨翁之恋惊世骇俗，如果他们没有 1995 年汕头大学的那次偶遇，茫茫人海中，两人断然不可能相见相知相悦相恋。我认为这就是缘分。

我要说的是“书缘”。在 20 世纪 90 年代中期，逛广州购书中心，看到一本英文原版书 *365 Love Poems*，心想，这本书很好，以后有空，每天读一首情诗，定会陶情适性、心驰神往。随手买下，一搁就是 20 年。直到 2015 年，敝人第二次退休，卸下身负的社会职务重担，才有空闲。此时，我的那本拙作，将传统营销学条分缕析做成工具书的《营销传播 A–Z》，已经处于校对付梓阶段，正思量接下来该做什么事好呢。我想到那本“365”，编选翻译一本爱情诗，可能还有市场。爱情这个文学永恒主题，毋庸赘言，当然也是男女老少须臾离不开的感情，人人都向往——爱人与被爱。正如莎士比亚所言：“我真幸福，既爱着人，又被人所爱。”（Then happy I, that love and am beloved.）

当年初秋，我到美国费城探亲。在当地书店，看看有什么可作为译材的原著，把全城书店跑了个遍。一天，逛到一家旧书店，店员是一位老者，一讲 love poem 这两个词，他马上指向二楼。登上狭窄的木梯，我看到一本 *1001 Love Poems*，喜出望外，心花怒放，厚厚一大本，正文有 704 个页码。这是最好的译材。

2016 年暮秋，我第二次赴美探亲。此时，我已经草译了一百多首情诗，想再看看有什么爱情诗集。我之所以破费买下同类书，几乎见到就买，因为自己要在浩如烟海的英文诗中挑选佳作，不如利用现成的已编辑出版的诗集，从中进一步比较挑选，可大大省劲。

所有爱情诗的英文选本，莎士比亚十四行诗是不可或缺的，而且，占有一定数量。上面提及的那本“1001”，竟然将莎翁 154 首十四行诗悉数选入。莎翁诗作 400 多年前写的，他的隐喻、双关语及其中古英语用法，要读懂，谈何容易！他的诗具有世俗性、戏剧性及洞察人情世故的深刻性，其后的浪漫主义诗歌有所不逮。在我经常去浏览的 Barnes&Noble 书店，刻意去莎士比亚著作书架上寻找。恰好有本玛格莱特·德·格雷西亚（Margreta de Grazia）编辑的《莎士比亚十四行诗》（*Shakespeare's Sonnets*，2011）。虽然每首诗只有不足一页的注释，粗略一看也够用了，我付款购得，心满意足地离开书店。

过了几天，我在住处附近名叫意大利市场的小区逛街。在一间不起眼的小店，我驻足一会儿，起先以为是买旧唱片的店，我从小门往里瞄去，看到一排排书架有不少的图书。进去后，走近书架，跳入眼帘的竟是一本厚厚的《莎士比亚十四行诗》*Shakespeare's*

Sonnets，耶鲁大学 1977 年版的，共 583 页，它的前半部是 1609 年初版的四开本影印文本及并列刊印的编辑文本，注解集中放在书的后半部，足足有 450 页，每首诗的分析注释详细得无以复加。这对我理解和翻译莎士比亚有极大助益。我在美国购买旧书已经有了一点经验，书的价钱及定价日期，店主一般是用铅笔在书籍扉页的右上角小字注明。此书写着“$7/12–10”，二手价 7 美元，与原价 19.95 美元相比，是绝对超值。卖书的女子笑容可掬，要知道，这书进店已有四年了，她终于见到我这个主顾，特意微笑着给了我两张书签。她怎知我内心的兴奋和激动胜过她多少倍呢！因为，这是惊喜，我事先根本不知道有这本书。这真正是“书缘”。不过，至今我不明白，这类书就像古籍的集注或会评本，应该在高等学府附近出售，怎会窝在肉菜市场里呢？

这本书确实管用。例如，莎翁十四行诗第 73 首，有个词组“death’s second self”，照字面上，可译为“死亡的影子”或“死亡的化身”。这本书注解是，这是“sleep”的常用的文艺复兴时期的别称，用于夜晚，引申指笼罩白天、紧闭眼睛，或封闭一切。显然，与死亡相去甚远。

幸亏有“书缘”，我在两年不到的时间内，搜集到十几本英文原版诗集，得以借助前人的成果而工作。现在，我从中选译了 98 首诗。包含 64 位诗人，时间跨度比较大，从 16 世纪直到 20 世纪 50 年代。每位诗人，无论他或她生于何时何地，都以新颖的和坦诚的方式探索爱情，每首诗反映不同的生活场景，表现不同的情绪感悟，呈现个人化的爱情观。爱情超越时间和国界。这些爱情诗都可能引起一部分读者的共鸣。本书由于作品数量不大，只是粗略地按主题编排顺序，大体是从爱情定义开始，经过认识、初恋、恋情、婚姻、分手，直到回忆。

译诗很难。甚至许多人说诗是不能翻译的。美国诗人弗罗斯特曾经有句名言：“诗是经过翻译丢失的东西。”因此，照这个说法，我不能收录英译的外文诗，因为，英译已丢失了一次诗意，我再次转译，那岂不是丢失殆尽。本选集的英诗作品大部分是格律诗。原原本本按照英文诗的格律翻译成汉语，如同将我国的古典诗词按照格律要求译成英文一样，我个人认为是几乎不可能的。我是个业余译者，没有高深的理论指导。我的译诗原则是，力求正确理解原诗内容，尽量用优美的中文表达出来。限于本人学识水平和翻译功力，本集的译诗尽可能在音步、韵式和行数上依照原诗。但在具体操作上，不拘泥原诗韵式，不会以韵害意，实在难以押韵的，索性不押，如果勉强硬凑韵脚，增字添词，跨行倒装，弄得削足适履，诘屈聱牙，最终仍然得不偿失。我认为，译诗是给当代中国人阅读的，押韵方面，也可照顾中国人的习惯，不必死硬照搬英文诗韵式。例如，英文诗多元化的韵脚，照搬译成中文，原诗的铿锵回旋的音乐性也不能体现。

诗歌翻译，对各国近代诗歌形式发展影响巨大。我国“五四”以来的新诗，显然，发轫于外国诗的引进。近些年有一项研究，颠覆我的固有认知，就是美国20世纪初期兴起的意象派诗或新诗，起源于我国古典诗词的影响。可见，文化的交流传播是双向的，经常互为因果。值得一提的是，许多英文爱情诗选本，都收有我国古人的作品，如杜甫、李白、李商隐、温庭筠等，最常选的一首是李白（Li Po) 的《长干行》（The River Merchant's Wife: A Letter），可能与译者名气有关，他是埃兹拉·庞德(1885–1972)，美国著名诗人，意象派的鼻祖。

诗的开头六句：“妾发初复额，折花门前剧。郎骑竹马来，绕床弄青梅。同居长干里，两小无嫌猜。”说的是女子回忆童年时“青梅竹马”“两小无猜”（本诗是这两个成语的出处）的情景。庞德的英译是：

While my hair was still cut straight across my forehead/I played about the front gate, pulling flowers./You came by on bamboo stilts, playing horse,/You walked about my seat, playing with blue plums./And we went on living in the village of Chokan/Two small people, without dislike or suspicion.

有论者说，庞德译作是将对中国诗的主观感受以优美的英文呈现出来，他重视的是对读者的美学感染力。庞德的译文已经公认为英美文学的翻译经典。庞德这种“创意性翻译”方法也值得我们借鉴。

我从事广告管理 30 多年。2016 年刚刚出版编译的《营销传播 A–Z》，转而翻译文学，好多朋友大惑不解。实际上，我早在 20 世纪 80 年代初期已经业余进行文学翻译了。当时利用业余时间到广东中山图书馆里外文部查阅、抄录资料。我读了不少馆藏旧书，如托马斯·哈代的诗集。哈代的诗沉郁、厚重、朴实风格吸引了我，我也早已脱离了青春期浪漫主义的爱好。我选译了一些，最后选择两首投稿：《老工人》（The Old Workman）和《希望之歌》（Song of Hope）。自以为这两首内容积极向上，符合无产阶级文学主旋律。

后来，在 1982 年第 2 期《译海》杂志上发表。远在美国的表哥程美生（Henry M.Cheng）得知后，一下子寄了十多本英文书。他以为我要以文学翻译为生了。他不知道，业余翻译可不能当饭吃。人生各为稻粱谋，人当先安身立命糊口为生。我虽然没有选择专业翻译的职业，但是这种青少年时期的文学梦始终蕴藏在心中，所谓“不忘初衷”。这里特别提到已故的美生表哥，他的厚望，我记忆犹新，怀念之情油然而生，在这里写上一笔，权当心香一瓣，告慰在天之灵。

毋庸讳言，诗集中诗歌大部分已经翻译介绍进来。我也疑惑，再将它们重译出版有没有必要呢？有些是名家的翻译，你能够超越吗？爱情诗集里的诗，多是公认的经典名诗，有的是甚至是耳熟能详、人人皆知的，若不包含进来，那是很大的缺憾。至于译文的水平好坏优劣之分，敬请读者品判。译界先进们有一种说辞，说翻译如同演奏，同一首曲子，每个演奏者理解、感觉、技巧不同，诠释和表达就各不相同。如果这种论调成立，以后的后进者应该有发挥自己才能的空间。当然，这些诗作经过自己的演绎和加工，的确有不同的心得体会和表现形式。这创造性工作，我不时也有“吟安一个字，拈断数茎须”的苦乐感。无论如何，我在这里，依然要郑重对早先翻译的先行者，表示由衷敬意。在文化传承中，后人都是跟着前人的脚印后起步的，而且又有天然的后发优势，这是无可置疑的。

本诗集采取英汉对照。考虑到现在能够直接阅读英文的人越来越多，欣赏英文诗最好的方式是将原文交给读者，一方面能更好理解领会原诗，另一方面也可以评估译诗的得失。殷切期待英语专家和读者不吝指教，提出批评。

如果这本诗集的作品，能够使人们，特别是初恋者、热恋者或失恋者，从中得到些许的启发、快感或慰藉，激发生活灵感，提升情感品位，并且，能够提高对英语爱好者的英语学习和英语作品的兴趣，作为一个译者，便是聊以自慰，平生愿足。就我个人而言，做些文字工作，翻译爱情诗，既可重温难以忘怀的青春岁月的情趣，也是自我消遣的一种生活方式，有益身心，不亦乐乎！

这本书出版，感谢出版社的责任编辑张晶晶女士，在图书内容、版式装帧和插画选择上，做了大量工作，促成这本书的顺利编辑出版。感谢许多亲朋好友同行给予关注及勉励，其中也有诸多年轻的美籍华人，以他们读诗的亲身体验，在原诗理解上给我帮助，恕不一一列名。非常感谢暨南大学教授杨先顺先生在百忙中慨然允诺作序。

爱的心灵咒语

A Reasonable Affliction